CITY GOURMET GUIDES

D0719452

Conceived by: Ennio Bazzoni
Texts: Maria Salemi
Translation: Anthony Brierley

Editing: Alissa Zavanella
Picture research: Silvia Martini
Design e realization: Francesco Bertini

Technical coordination: Paola Bianchi
Colour reproduction: Fotolito Toscana, Firenze

CITY GOURMET GUIDES

FLORENCE

Traditional recipes
and gastronomic culture

NARDINI EDITORE

HISTORY

Ancient banquets: the eating habits of the Etruscans and Romans

The area in which the Roman settlement of *Florentia* would be founded in the 1st century BC was populated in antiquity by a great civilization, that of the Etruscans, whose art – tomb frescoes depicting scenes of hunting, fishing, banqueting and cooking, sculptures, reliefs and other objects found in excavations – reveals the important role played by gastronomy in the culture. Roasted meats, bean soups, cereal-meal mush, eggs and vegetables, legumes and cheeses, fish, fruit and condiments prepared with mortar-ground herbs made up a healthy yet refined diet, invariably washed down with the fine wine that was already being produced in Tuscany at this time.

These foods were subsequently inherited by the Romans, who continued to eat sober, appetizing dishes until a time when the expansion of their influence in the world aroused in wealthier

citizens the curiosity to try out more exotic and sometimes highly expensive foods. Ordinary folk, and all those who did not share this craving for originality and ostentation, this tendency toward luxury and extravagance, continued instead to consume the humble fare of traditional dishes, accompanied by wine flavoured with aromatic herbs, beer and mead, a mixture of water and fermented honey.

Innovation at the market-place and in the kitchen

In the 5th century AD the invasion of warrior peoples from the East and North led to the fall of the Roman Empire and the suppression of its civilization, including its gastronomic culture. The taste for good food and fine dining would flourish again only when order was re-established in the 12th century, when roads were again plied by travellers, pilgrims and merchants, and money began to flow again thanks to the revival of trade, fairs, markets and activities of all kinds.

As goods flowed into Florence from far-off lands, the countryside around the city became more intensively cultivated, vineyards and olive trees were planted and livestock-rearing became more widespread. The economic revival and an improvement in social welfare was accompanied by more refined customs and a yearning to enjoy the pleasures of life: at the table, therefore, there were expectations of greater quality, variety, and a new kind of refinement in the preparation and presentation of foods.

Into the city flowed olive oil produced in Tuscany, calves from the Val di Pesa and the Val di Chiana, chickens from the Valdarno, lambs from the Casentino and the Maremma, sea, lake and river fish, vegetables and legumes from the countryside, and wines from Chianti, Montalcino, Montepulciano and Elba. Kitchens and tables were enriched with new utensils and receptacles, and the most important families vied with each other in staging banquets in the city's squares or main streets for some illustrious guest. It is said that the episode which triggered the long and bloody feud between Guelphs and Ghibellines took place in 1225 when two young aristocrats, contending a platter laden with roasted meat, resorted to their daggers.

Old recipes for modern palates

As a result of the importance assumed by gastronomy, the first norms relating to the conduct of diners and table service were established, and the first cookery books appeared. Among them were the recipes collected in the 14th century by an anonymous Tuscan writer – complex and elaborate dishes, but also extremely simple

9

systems for cooking vegetables, legumes and wild herbs – some of which have survived in modern Florentine cuisine: ravioli, tortelli, maccheroni, pastry flans and timbale, fish, savoury and sweet pies and biscuits. With certain modifications, of course, since at this time there was a widespread use of sweet-sour, sweet-piquant and sweet-salty flavourings (today considered excessive), of sugar, almonds, raisins and spices: prized ingredients, the real status symbols of a society which even at the table could make a show of power.

Fourteenth-century cuisine, however, appears to be rich and varied, especially for the healthy and well-to-do. Oil and lard were used to cook dishes based on game, veal, lamb, pork, poultry and fish; grated Parmigiano was used to accompany ravioli and maccheroni; wine and vinegar was used in the preparation of stews and broths. Sensible, parsimonious Florentines ate simple dishes even when they had invited guests: stomach

of veal, boiled partridge, stewed sardines, boiled salted meat, tunafish with cabbage and, above all, legumes. Festive banquets were the occasion for spit-roasted quails, stuffed goose, vegetable and meat pies, sauces enriched with almonds and sugar, cakes and biscuits, candied fruits and spiced wines. And while the city Priors, the supreme rulers of the Republic, could afford to eat the best foods and already dined with silver cutlery at a time when most people continued to eat with their hands, the poor had to content themselves with dreaming of the fabulous Land of Plenty, with its rivers of wine, its "vine tendrils tied with sausages", its mountains of ravioli and maccheroni that everyone could eat freely, and the already roasted geese that fell from the sky.

Court banquets, tavern food and cooking as an art form

Opulence, variety and festivity were the hallmark of Florentine banqueting during the Renaissance period. But more than the lavish food served up on the bright orange-yellow and deep blue glazed earthenware dishes of the Medicean workshops of Cafaggiolo, Lorenzo the Magnificent loved the fare of the city's taverns, of which he was an assiduous visitor: simple, genuine food whose praises he sung in many of his works in verse, from the poems of *I beoni* and *La Nencia da Barberino* to the *Canti carnascialeschi*.

His successors, instead, followed the example of other Italian courts in preferring dishes that were amazing to look at but less amazing to consume, ingenious architectural masterpieces that were excessive in shape and colour and whose prime aim seemed to be that of drawing an applause from the admiring diners.

This model was reproduced with eccentricity by certain communities of artists in Florence (the Compagnia del Paiuolo and the Confraternita della Cazzuola), who amused themselves by staging banquets that were remarkable in their invention and realization. Many men of culture, like Anton Francesco Grazzini, known as "Lasca", Agnolo Tori, known as "Bronzino", Benedetto Varchi and Fiorenzuola, took pleasure instead in composing verses in praise of simple foods like omelettes, sausages, soups and melons.

11

Queens at the oven and in the pantry

Here we should tell the story of Caterina dei Medici. In 1533 the young princess married Henry II of France by proxy and departed for Paris with a hundred trunks of personal belongings, jewel-cases and a sumptuous retinue that included pastry-cooks, cellarmen, wine-servers and a master cook. The future queen of France had been raised as an orphan in Rome and later in Florence, where she had been entrusted to the care of the Dominican nuns of Santa Lucia and the Benedictine nuns of the Murate, famous for their rich spice shop, tasty sweets and perfumed elixirs. It was this early experience, as well as the greediness which earned her the nickname "venerable Idleness queen of Cockaigne", that contributed to Caterina's reputation as the cook who revived French cuisine with Florentine recipes. To her, in fact, goes the merit of having brought to northern Europe Tuscan beans, a certain liking for offal and fried foods, duck with orange sauce, savoury crepes, *salsa colla* or "glue sauce" (later known as *béchamel*), Frangipani cake (after the name of the gentleman in her retinue who had invented it), and of having revived the popularity of spinach, artichoke and parsley.

Legend has it that another member of the Medici family, Maria, also married by proxy to a French king, Henry IV, was responsible for introducing to France various Florentine specialities like pasta frolla (short pastry), creams, the pastry used to make bignè (cream puffs), and sherbets of milk and honey.

Florentine cuisine speaks French

As court cuisine became increasingly contrived and spectacular, the Florentine bourgeoisie of the 17th century maintained the costly simplicity that we discover by looking curiously into old recipe books like that of the Bardi, the powerful banking family, or of Giovanni del Turco, a gourmet and amateur cook as well as musician who was highly esteemed at the Medici court.

The last representatives of the Medici family paid little heed to food, and foreign influences increasingly appeared on their tables: French above all, but also English and Spanish. This tendency became more accentuated with the Austrian Lorraines, who succeeded them in the government of Tuscany, and with the House of Savoy which, after the unification of Italy, moved their court to Florence in the years 1865-71.

Thus, up until the first decade of the following century, at important banquets the lists of the dining courses were written in French, the recipes were French, the wines were French, and so too often were the cooks, who were contended by aristocratic families, restaurants and hotels, as an unequivocal mark of distinction.

'Trattorie', itinerant vendors and celebrated cooks

At the turn of last century we witness a real flowering of gastronomic publications: recipes were written not only by cooks of obvious fame and experience, but also by renowned journalists like Jarro and artists like Guido Peyron.

At the same time there was an improvement in the food of bourgeois families, who could profitably consult what was and still is the most famous Italian cook-book, *Science in the Kitchen and the Art of Eating Well* by Pellegrino Artusi, a collection of recipes largely inspired by Florentine cuisine. And there was of course still the excellent food of the city's old 'trattorie'.

14

The oldest was the 'Osteria delle Bertucce', object of the gastronomic forays of Lorenzo il Magnifico. Years later saw the opening of the 'Osteria del Porco', those of the 'Fico', 'Cervia', 'Agnolo', 'Vinegia', 'Malvasia' and, in modern times, the 'Osteria della Baldracca', 'Beppe Sudicio', 'Gigi Porco', 'La Luna', 'La Vecchia Vespa' and 'Le Antiche Carrozze'. Up to the time of the 'Troia', the 'Coco Lezzone', the 'Antico Fattore' and the 'Cave di Maiano', the Melini tavern and the dearly remembered Sabatini tavern-wine bar.

Firenze
Barroccio del vino
(Costumi Toscani)

15

In the popular eating-houses there were simple soups and stewed salt cod, beans in tomato sauce and cured pork sausage. And, if in the basements of houses and *palazzi* expensive tourist "holes" had opened up, the locals frequented the 'rosticceria della Fila', the first in Florence, with its sucking calf that could "raise the dead from their graves", and the stalls selling tripe and offal, black pudding, frogs and lamb's heads, herrings and salt cod, scattered about the streets and above all in the Mercato Vecchio, in the area of present-day Piazza della Repubblica. A sad loss, perpetrated in the name of hygiene and progress, and made worse by the slow disappearance of typical *vinai* (wine-bars) and *trattorie* which have been overwhelmed by sandwich-bars and fast-food shops.

"Cooking is a roguish thing; it so often makes you despair, but also gives pleasure, for on those occasions when you succeed and overcome some difficulty, you can feel satisfied and exult in your victory". Artusi dedicated these reflections to the practice of cooking, thus encouraging all those who, like the Florentines, can at all times obtain fresh food, cold-pressed olive oil and wines that are among the finest in Italy: ingredients of the highest quality with which to continue the gastronomic tradition with fidelity, good taste and love.

Pancotto
BREAD SOUP

✍ 250 g of stale household bread* cut into thin slices; 2 cloves of garlic cut in half; 8 spoonfuls of grated Parmigiano, in addition to that on the table; one litre of salt water; 4 spoonfuls of extra virgin olive oil; salt

✍ *Preparation: 10' - Cooking time: 25'*

✍ Heat the water. As soon as it boils add the bread and the garlic and cook, mixing for 15'. Blend in the oil and the Parmigiano and stir well for a few minutes before removing from the heat. Sprinkle with Parmigiano and serve warm with a dash of olive oil.

Pappa al pomodoro
BREAD AND TOMATO SOUP

✍ 300 g of stale household bread* cut into thin slices; 500 g of ripe tomatoes cut into pieces without skins or pips; a bunch of coarsely cut basil leaves; a pinch of chilli pepper; one litre of hot vegetable broth; 4 spoonfuls of extra virgin olive oil; salt; pepper

✍ *Preparation: 20' - Cooking time: 15' in addition to the time for leaving the mush*

✍ Gently sauté the garlic and chilli pepper in the oil; when they have taken on colour, add the tomatoes, basil and bread. Turn up the heat and cook for 5', pour in the broth and cook for 5' from the moment it boils. You should obtain a dense mush that should be left for at least half an hour. Before serving, stir well and add a dash of oil and a sprinkling of pepper.

➳ *This is one of the many versions of a famous dish, excellent whether hot or cold. It can vary according to the quantities of the ingredients, then there are those who use a lot of garlic, those who replace it with leek, or an onion, or with all the 'odori'*; those who boil all the ingredients together, those who toss the already cooked tomatoes into the boiling broth together with the garlic and the lightly toasted bread, then beat everything with a whisk to make a purée.*

∾ 1 ∾

LET NOTHING GO TO WASTE

At the time of the Medici one ate enough for sixteen; at the time of the Lorraines, breakfast, lunch and dinner; today, with progress, just a thin soup and a little boiled meat.

(popular Florentine saying)

So went a popular saying of the early 20th century, when a thin broth or a stew with a little meat and a lot of potatoes was a rare luxury for common folk. Yet even in times of widespread prosperity Florentine cuisine remains a "poor" one, made up of simple, essential, wholesome foods flavoured with laurel and herbs.

A tradition that does not misuse ingredients and mixtures, that abhors waste, that is best expressed in the few surviving *trattorie* and *fiaschetterie* (taverns), the authentic ones, not those invented by recent fashions indulgent towards various other *cuisines, nouvelles* or otherwise, that have come from afar.

A cuisine consisting frequently of lengthy cooking times, or even "re-cooking", of stale bread softened in water, of entrails, of scraps. Modest food that in terms of flavour and harmony rivals that made with costly, prized ingredients inherited from Medicean cuisine or created by cooks in the service of aristocratic or well-to-do families, restaurants, hotels or private circles.

A cuisine in which the thick, rich beef steak, the glorious "bistecca alla fiorentina", represents an unexpected and prodigious anomaly.

Panzanella
BREAD AND VEGETABLE SALAD

🌀 600 g of stale household bread* cut into thick slices; 6 thinly sliced ripe tomatoes; 2 red onions (or, in summer, 4 thinly sliced fresh onions); 2 good handfuls of fresh basil, hand-broken into small pieces; 3 spoonfuls of extra virgin olive oil; a dash of good red wine vinegar; salt

🌀 *Preparation: 30'*

🌀 While you prepare the vegetables, soak the bread in cold water. When it is soft and swollen, scoop a handful at a time, squeeze it well so that it remains just damp and break it up into small pieces. Blend it with the vegetables, add the dressing, and mix together using your hands.

🍽 *You can garnish with onion rings, tomato slices and basil leaves.*
The pepper is optional, as is the addition of other ingredients to vary the taste: slices of celery or cucumber, aromatic herbs (parsley, calamint, thyme…), lettuce, tuna, anchovies and so on.

Minestra di pane

BREAD AND BEAN SOUP

✍ 700 g of boiled fresh white cannellini beans* (or 300 g if dry); 300 g of skinned tomatoes chopped into pieces; half a savoy cabbage, cut thinly; a bunch of black cabbage (without ribs and well washed), cut into pieces; 4 good slices of toasted household bread* rubbed with a clove of garlic; a finely chopped mixture of: one red onion, one stick of celery, a handful of parsley, one piece of chilli pepper; 2 dl of the water the beans cooked in; 6 spoonfuls of extra virgin olive oil; salt; pepper

✍ *Preparation:* 20' - *Cooking time:* 1 h

✍ Fry the finely chopped mixture in the oil; when it starts to brown blend in the tomatoes, salt and cook on a low flame for about 10'. Then add the cabbage and beans, half whole and half passed through a sieve, together with their cooking water. Simmer* for 45' and pour over the garlic bread; garnish with a dash of oil.

🍃 *This traditional meatless soup can be flavoured with the addition of a slice of lard in the finely chopped mixture or by cooking together with the beans either a bone of ham stripped of its meat, or pieces of pigskin. An excellent variation involves replacing the bread with pasta or rice.*

Ribollita
THICK BREAD AND VEGETABLE SOUP

ↄ 500 g of household bread*, at least two days old; 700 g of boiled fresh cannellini beans* (or 300 g if dry); half a savoy cabbage, finely chopped; 2 bunches of black cabbage (without ribs and well washed), cut into pieces; a small bunch of chard; 2 ripe tomatoes cut into pieces, without skins or pips; one red onion and one clove of garlic, finely chopped; 2 sticks of celery; 2 carrots; one leek; a sprig of thyme; the water the beans cooked in; 8 spoonfuls of extra virgin olive oil; salt; pepper

ↄ *Preparation:* 45' - *Cooking time:* 2 h and 10'

ↄ As you pass through the sieve ¾ of the beans with their water, fry the garlic and onion in an earthenware pot. When they start to brown, add the chopped celery, carrots and leek. Cook for an hour on a low flame, then add the other vegetables, thyme, salt and pepper. Add the sieved beans and simmer* for another hour, stirring well. A few minutes before removing from the heat, stir in the whole beans. Pour the soup into an earthenware receptacle, alternating with layers of bread, and leave for 24 hours.

ↄ *This is clearly one of the many meatless soups of the popular tradition. To carry the glorious title of "ribollita" it must be recooked for a long time with more oil. At one time it was customary, every Friday, to prepare large quantities of it so that it could be eaten for breakfast on Saturday morning.*

Francesina o lesso rifatto

FRENCH STEW (BOILED BEEF WITH ONIONS)

ᴄᴧᴼ 500 g of boiled meat* in small pieces or slices; 800 g of finely sliced onions; 500 g of ripe chopped tomatoes, without skins or pips; 2 cloves of garlic; 3-4 leaves of sage; a spoonful of flour (optional); half a cup of red wine (optional); 4 spoonfuls of extra virgin olive oil; salt; freshly ground pepper (or, if preferred, chilli pepper)

ᴄᴧᴼ *Preparation: 20' - Cooking time: 20'*

ᴄᴧᴼ Sauté the garlic and sage in the oil, add the onions and tomatoes, salt, pepper and cook for about 10'. Add the stewing meat (if preferred it can be coated in flour), steep with the wine and cook on a low heat for another 10', stirring often.

ᒂ✍ *A simpler version involves simmering* the pieces of boiled meat* for 10' in the onions that have been sautéed and cooked together with the tomatoes or with 2 spoonfuls of concentrate dissolved in a little water. Another version uses a lightly fried mixture of streaky bacon, onion, carrot and celery in which to sauté the meat for about 10', which must then be steeped in red wine and cooked for 15' together with the chopped tomatoes, and for another 10' with a handful of dried mushrooms soaked in warm water and finely chopped.*

Polpette, polpettone, braciole rifatti

RISSOLES, MEATLOAF, REHEATED CUTLETS

ᓫᓫᓬ 4 fried cutlets (or 8 slices of meatloaf or 12 rissoles); 2 cloves of crushed garlic; a sprig of parsley chopped with a clove of garlic; 500 g of tomatoes, skinned and chopped; 4 spoonfuls of extra virgin olive oil; salt; pepper

ᓫᓫᓬ *Preparation: 20' - Cooking time: 30'*

ᓫᓫᓬ Lightly fry the garlic and parsley in the oil. When they start to brown, add the tomatoes. Salt, pepper and cook on a low flame for 10'. Put in the meat and cook for about 15 minutes over a low flame so that they become tender again and acquire flavour.

ᓫᓫᓬ *A rapid version involves adding 200 g of tomato sauce to the fried garlic and parsley: as soon as it boils, immerse the meat in it for a few minutes and serve hot. Fried cutlets are excellent also bathed in hot anchovy sauce and, with 'braciole alla fiorentina', cut into small pieces and heated in their sauce, can be used to garnish a dish of pasta.*

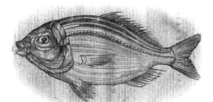

Polpette di baccalà

SALT COD FRITTERS

ᓫᓫᓬ 400 g of boiled salt cod chopped up together with 6 fillets of anchovy; 200 g of stale bread* soaked in a cup of milk and squeezed; half a clove of garlic; a small handful of parsley leaves, chopped; one egg; 150 g of breadcrumbs; a lemon for garnishing; plenty of frying oil; salt; pepper

ᓫᓫᓬ *Preparation: 15' - Cooking time: 15'*

ᓫᓫᓬ Break the egg in a bowl and blend in the bread, the chopped anchovies and salt cod, the garlic and the parsley. Taste for salt and pepper and roll the mixture into small balls. Coat them in breadcrumbs and fry. Serve them either hot or cold, garnished with slices of lemon.

Fiori di zucca ripieni
STUFFED COURGETTE FLOWERS

ᏬᎧ 12 very fresh and fairly large courgette flowers; 150 g of boiled or stewed mincemeat; 70 g of bechamel sauce; one beaten egg; a sprig of chopped parsley; batter*; plenty of frying oil

ᏬᎧ *Preparation:* 30' - *Cooking time:* 15'

ᏬᎧ Wash the flowers and carefully remove the pistil and small green sepals around the corolla. Then prepare the stuffing: blend the meat with the bechamel sauce and parsley, bind with the egg and season with salt and pepper. Stuff the flowers with this mixture, dip them into a fairly runny batter and, after letting them drip, fry them, turning carefully so that they golden evenly. Serve hot and crispy.

ᎨᎦ *These flowers can also be filled with mozzarella cheese, anchovy and bread soaked in milk and wrung out (with or without bechamel). Or otherwise with a mixture of garlic, ricotta, Parmigiano, bacon and nutmeg bound with egg. Whatever the stuffing, if they get left over, they can be very tasty cooked again in tomato sauce seasoned with garlic and parsley.*

Involtini di cavolo
STUFFED CABBAGE LEAVES

🌀 12 large tender leaves of a savoy cabbage; 400 g of minced boiled meat*; 300 g of puréed ripe tomatoes; one egg; one clove of garlic; a sprig of chopped parsley; 2 spoonfuls of grated Parmigiano; 8 spoonfuls of extra virgin olive oil; salt; pepper; chilli pepper (optional)

🌀 *Preparation:* 30' - *Cooking time:* 1 h

🌀 Boil the cabbage leaves in plenty of salt water (about 10' from the time the water starts to boil). Drain them and lay them out on a cloth to dry. In the meantime prepare the stuffing by mixing the meat with the egg and the chopped parsley and garlic. Season with salt and pepper. Put a spoonful of this mixture on each leaf and wrap it up tightly pressing firmly with the hands. Close the bundles by piercing them with a tooth-pick and cook for another 20' on a low flame in a covered pan. Lastly, add the tomatoes and cook for another 20'.
Excellent either hot or cold with a sprinkling of Parmigiano.

Frittata col lesso
BOILED MEAT OMELETTE

୧୨ 200 g of chopped boiled meat*;
4 beaten eggs; a piece of ham fat; a small bunch
of sage leaves; 2 spoonfuls of extra virgin olive
oil; salt

୧୨ *Preparation:* 10' - *Cooking time:* 15'

୧୨ Oil a pan with the ham fat, add the oil,
the sage and the boiled meat. Salt and lightly
cook the mixture without letting it brown.
Pour in the slightly salted eggs, turn up the heat
and fry over a low flame, turning over halfway
through the cooking.

*Leftovers of boiled meat can also be used to make
tasty rissoles: chop the pieces finely and mix into them
a mashed boiled potato or a small handful of soft
bread soaked in milk and wrung out, a clove of garlic
chopped up with parsley, grated Parmigiano, salt and
pepper. Make small balls or rissoles out of the mixture,
coat them in breadcrumbs or flour and fry them in hot
oil. The same mixture can be used to fill the boiled
leaves of a savoy cabbage, which you can wrap up and
fasten with a toothpick before putting them in the oven
with oil, salt, pepper and broth or, if preferred, tomato.*

26

TASTY SAVOURIES

*Florentines eat so sparingly and so simply
that they always keep up a good appetite.*

(popular Florentine saying)

We are certainly no longer accustomed to it.
And yet until a few decades ago the courses of
important meals followed each other in endless
succession, according to a precise order that
varied from area to area and from countryside
to city. In Florence a lunch would begin with a
watery soup to open the stomach and prepare it
for the meal proper. Starters were, in fact, served
after it, followed by the *fritto* (or by stewed or
boiled meat), by the *rifreddo* (galantine or
gelatine cold meats, with tunny-fish sauce, in
pies), by the *trasmesso* (or middle course, with
hot savoury pies, bread slices with savouries,
timbale, stuffed vegetables), by roast meat, by
vegetables and by dessert (sweets, fresh and dried
fruit, cheese). We have preferred, then, to
replace the "starters" chapter with one that also
includes additional recipes suitable for quick
tasty snacks and rustic aperitifs. In keeping,
therefore, with our increasingly rushed lifestyle,
but not to the detriment of quality or tradition.
Raw vegetable salads, tripe, ham and melon, can
be served with a cold dry white wine, still or
sparkling, perfumed and not too structured.
Ham, salami, crostini, coccoli and fettunta are
best accompanied by young, fruity red wines; fish
by fragrant, aromatic rosé wines. Instead, artichokes, pickled vegetables, pickled fish, bread
salad and, in general, all dishes tasting of vinegar
or lemon, should not be eaten with any wine.

Fettunta

TOASTED BREAD SLICES WITH OLIVE OIL

ɹ 6 good-sized long slices of stale household bread*, one finger thick and with the crust; one clove of peeled garlic; plenty of extra virgin olive oil; salt; freshly ground black pepper

ɹ *Preparation:* 5' in addition to the time for heating the grill - *Cooking time:* 15'

ɹ Grill the bread slices carefully, making sure that they come out crunchy on the outside but are still soft in the middle. Rub garlic on the slices and serve very hot, sprinkled with salt and pepper and with a generous coating of oil.

ɹ *These appetizing and great smelling slices of bread – which can be topped with marzolino cheese in spring, with tomato and basil leaves for a refreshing summer snack, but also with white beans boiled with garlic, sage and bayleaf, or with boiled black cabbage leaves and a sprinkling of lemon juice – have secrets that it is as well to know in order to make them perfect. They should, for example, be roasted over charcoal, better still if of vine or olive wood to aromatize them, and garnished with oil* that must be Tuscan, cold pressed and possibly "novo" (i.e. straight from the mill). And young red wine, and the cheer of a warm fireplace.*

28

Coccoli

BREAD DOUGH FRITTERS

✿ 400 g of flour; 40 g of brewer's yeast dissolved in a cup of lukewarm water; 40 g of lard (or, if preferred, butter); salt; plenty of frying oil

✿ *Preparation:* 10' in addition to the time needed for the dough to rise and 10' for making up the balls - *Cooking time:* 30'

✿ Pour the yeast into the centre of the flour heaped on a pastry-board with a well in the middle. Add the lard and knead it until a soft elastic ball is formed which should be left to rise for a couple of hours in a warm place. Then with flour-dusted hands, make small balls with a diameter of about 2 cm and fry them in the boiling oil. When they have puffed up and are golden, drain them and leave them to dry on kitchen paper. Serve them very hot, sprinkled with salt.

✿ *Fried bread dough, either sweet or salty, is a humble yet exquisite food in use in many regions of Italy. A food with no pretensions, it can also be easily made with yeast powder (which does not require the dough to be left to rise) or even with pizza dough bought from a baker's shop.*
In Florence they can still be bought in some 'friggitoria' (fried-food shop) in the area of the Mercato Centrale, sold in a piece of thick yellow paper greasy with frying oil. Their name derives from the cypress berries which they resemble; but they were also called "galletti" (little cocks), because of the little fried peduncle resembling a beak that is formed when tossing the ball into the oil, or "sommommoli" (punches), because they can look like little closed fists.

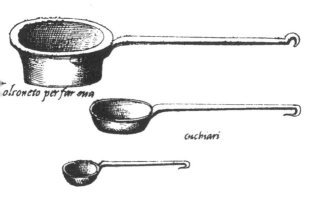

olsoneto per far ous

cuchiari

Tondone
FRIED BATTER ROUNDS

🌀 A thick batter* prepared with: 100 g of flour and a cup of water; salt; plenty of frying oil

🌀 *Preparation:* 5' in addition to the 30' for leaving the batter - *Cooking time:* 15'

🌀 Pour the batter into the boiling oil with the help of a ladle and cook until golden on both sides. Drain and leave to dry on a piece of kitchen paper. Serve with Tuscan salumi*.

🌿 *Excellent whether hot or cold, today it is an appetizing snack, although at one time it was often used to give substance to a light evening meal. In times that were not too hard an egg could be added to the batter and it was eaten with ham or blood sausage. For a more aromatic version chop bayleaves very finely and add to the batter: "old" leaves, possibly harder than the buds, but full of perfume and flavour.*

Salvia fritta
FRIED SAGE LEAVES

🌀 36 large sage leaves, carefully washed and dried; 4-5 anchovies, desalted and filleted, chopped into small pieces; a runny batter* prepared with: water, beer and salt; plenty of frying oil

🌀 *Preparation:* 20' - *Cooking time:* 15'

🌀 After having put every little piece of anchovy between two leaves, press them hard so they stick together, dip them into the batter and fry them in the hot (not boiling) oil. Drain them, dry them on a piece of kitchen paper and serve hot.

🌿 *It is advisable to prepare these appetizing fritters (of which a version exists without anchovies) in late spring, when the sage leaves are fresh, full of aroma and very tender. This very old recipe comes from the Middle Ages, a period when it was customary to fry just about everything: cheese and eggs, flowers and fruit, fish, meat and vegetables, young vine tendrils, rice, tender young bayleaves, sprigs of rosemary and more.*

Crostini di fegatini di pollo

TOASTED BREAD WITH CHICKEN LIVER PASTE

ɛ◠ 500 g of stale bread*, toasted, cut into slices and moistened in the broth*; 300 g of chicken livers, stripped of the whitish filaments and gall bladders, washed and dried; half a litre of broth; one small red onion, chopped finely; a heaped spoonful of pickled capers, well squeezed and chopped; one filleted anchovy (optional); half a cup of dry Vinsanto (or white wine); 3 spoonfuls of extra virgin olive oil; salt; pepper

ɛ◠ *Preparation:* 15' in addition to the 10' for making up the crostini - *Cooking time:* 30'

ɛ◠ Sauté the onion in the oil, put in the livers and half cook them, adding the Vinsanto little by little and stirring regularly. Remove from the heat, chop finely and complete the cooking, bathing in the broth. Add the capers and, as desired, the anchovy; salt, pepper and blend well. Spread this cream onto the dry side of the bread and serve the crostini hot or cold.

ɜ☙ *There are many variations of this classic recipe, not all of them universally accepted. The initial fry mixture may include leeks and celery or shallots or all the 'odori'*, sometimes with the addition of a spoonful of tomato sauce and perhaps a little butter or ham fat; instead of Vinsanto some use white wine or even Marsala; and, if to the capers a couple of fillets of well desalted anchovy are often added, there are those who prefer to replace them with dried mushrooms soaked in water and then chopped finely.*

Collo ripieno
STUFFED CHICKEN'S NECK

✎ 2 necks of chicken, plucked and deboned; 200 g of minced veal; 100 g of minced pork; 100 g of grated Parmigiano; 50 g of butter; 3 eggs; a fistful of bread soaked in milk and squeezed; a grating of nutmeg; a sprig of thyme; a bunch of 'odori'* for the broth; salt; pepper

✎ *Preparation:* 30' in addition to the time for deboning and plucking the necks, a laborious operation that it would be easier to ask of the poulterer - *Cooking time:* 40'

✎ Sauté the meat with the butter and thyme, let it cool and then pass it through the mixer to obtain a creamy, homogeneous paste. Add the other ingredients and mix everything well. Sew up one end of the necks and stuff them, being careful not to overfill them, then sew up the other end. Prick the neck skins here and there with a fork and immerse them in salt water brought to the boil with the 'odori'. Simmer* for about 30', remove from the heat and leave them to go warm. Serve in thin slices with pickles*.

✎ *A tasty variation sees the thyme substituted by a pinch of chopped parsley and a smattering of grated lemon peel. And, for those who like it, a small amount of garlic.*

Insalata di trippa
TRIPE SALAD

✎ 400 g of washed boiled tripe*, chopped into very thin strips; 100 g of stoned black olives, chopped into pieces; one small red onion, finely sliced; a sprig of chopped parsley; extra virgin olive oil; salt; freshly ground black pepper

✎ *Preparation:* 20'

✎ Combine the tripe with all the other ingredients, add the dressing, mix well and store in a cool place before serving.

✎ *This refreshing dish lends itself to the addition of numerous other ingredients: pickled vegetables, cooked ham, finely chopped onion, basil and parsley (or chilli pepper, garlic and parsley), beans, spring onions, celery and potatoes. Even the dressing can be enriched with vinegar and mustard or a few drops of lemon.*

Insalata "di Caterina"
CATERINA'S SALAD

ᒓᘀ Very fresh misticanza*; 50 g of diced Tuscan pecorino cheese; 2 boiled eggs, cut into segments; 4 fillets of anchovy in olive oil, chopped into small pieces; one spoonful of capers; extra virgin olive oil; good red wine vinegar; salt; pepper

ᒓᘀ *Preparation:* 15'

ᒓᘀ Clean and wash the herbs, dry them well and put them in a soup-serving bowl. Add the Tuscan pecorino cheese, the anchovy and the spoonful of capers. Salt, pepper and dress with oil and vinegar, mix well and garnish with the segments of boiled egg.

ᶜᕽ *The name of this salad, also called "Renaissance salad", comes from the popular belief that Caterina de' Medici was extremely fond of it. In fact it is a relatively modern creation, the addition of pecorino cheese making it a "shepherd's salad".*

Pesce finto
FALSE FISH

○ Half kg of yellow mealy potatoes, boiled and passed through a mouli; 250 g of tunafish in olive oil, drained and broken up into pieces; 2 spoonfuls of mayonnaise; 2 spoonfuls of capers (or a cluster of parsley), chopped; salt; pepper. For the garnish: 10 pickled gherkins or fresh little carrots cut into thin roundels; one black olive; a strip of red bell pepper

○ *Cooking time:* 20'-30' for boiling the potatoes - *Preparation:* 30' in addition to the time needed for them to cool down

○ Mix together the tunafish, the potatoes, the mayonnaise and the capers (or parsley). Adjust salt and pepper. Give the mixture the shape of a fish and cover it with the roundels of gherkin or carrot to resemble scales. The olive can be used for the eye, the pepper for the mouth and tail fin.

You can also cover it simply with mayonnaise, boiled egg cut into roundels and pickled vegetables*, although if you prepare it some hours in advance, protect it with a generous coating of brandy-flavoured vegetal gelatine.
Tunafish was an important resource in days of shortage, that is, when the Church ordered people to abstain from eating meat. With a fine glass of Chianti the Florentines could consume it habitually on the counters of wine-shops, as an alternative to hard-boiled eggs, often accompanied by beans* boiled and garnished with red onions cut into very thin slices, oil from the mill, salt and a sprinkling of freshly ground pepper.

Pomodori al forno
STUFFED TOMATOES

🕭 4 round, fleshy, perfectly ripe tomatoes; 200 g of Arborio rice, boiled *al dente*; 100 g of chopped mozzarella cheese; one beaten egg; some fresh basil leaves, chopped finely; 100 g of butter; grated Parmigiano; extra virgin olive oil; salt; pepper

🕭 *Preparation:* 20' in addition to the time needed for the rice to cool down - *Cooking time:* 25' for boiling the rice and 20' in the oven

🕭 Pour the rice into boiling salt water and, while it is cooking, cut the tomatoes horizontally in such a way as to obtain a deep cup and a "lid". Empty them, drain them of their own juice, and sprinkle them with salt and pepper.
Mix into the cold rice the "lid" chopped up into pieces, the mozzarella cheese and the basil; salt, pepper, and bind with the egg. Fill the tomato cups with this mixture, sprinkle with cheese, add a dash of oil and flakes of butter and gratinate in a hot oven.

🕭 *Also excellent are small tomatoes simply garnished with oil, salt and basil, and cooked in a low oven for 45'. Or the "summer" variety, filled with chopped tunafish mixed together with anchovy fillets, capers, chopped parsley or basil and, if desired, a couple of cloves of garlic.*

Aringa marinata
PICKLED HERRING

🕭 2 salted female herrings (i.e. with eggs), washed and filleted; a very finely chopped mixture of: 2 carrots, one spring onion, one stick of celery, a pinch of black peppercorns (or 2 dried chilli peppers); half a cup of extra virgin olive oil

🕭 *Preparation:* 15'

🕭 Lay the herrings over the finely chopped vegetables, cover with oil and leave for 24 hours. Serve with fresh or toasted Tuscan bread*, with boiled potatoes or with a slice of polenta.

Baccalà marinato
PICKLED SALT COD

⌒ 800 g of salt cod* soaked in water, deboned and cut into pieces; 2 ripe tomatoes, cut into pieces, without skins or pips; 2 cloves of garlic; one spoonful of parsley leaves; a sprig of rosemary; 3 dried chilli peppers; 4 spoonfuls of flour; half a cup of good red wine vinegar (mixed with water if too strong); 3 spoonfuls of extra virgin olive oil; plenty of frying oil; one lemon to garnish

⌒ *Preparation:* 15' in addition to the time for cooling the sauce - *Cooking time:* 40'

⌒ Coat the fish pieces in flour and fry them on both sides. Remove from the pan and lay in a terrine. In the same oil fry the garlic, add the other ingredients and simmer* for 10'. Remove from the heat and leave to cool. Pour the sauce over the fish and leave for the whole day. Decorate with slices of lemon.

Acciughe marinate
PICKLED ANCHOVIES

⌒ One kg of fresh anchovies, washed, devoid of head, tail, entrails and bones; a finely chopped mixture of: 4 cloves of garlic, one chilli pepper, a small bunch of parsley, a pinch of peppercorns; half a litre of good wine vinegar; a dash of extra virgin olive oil; salt; pepper

⌒ *Preparation:* 30'

⌒ Lay the anchovies in layers in a glass jar with an air-tight lid, sprinkling over each layer salt, pepper and the chopped herb mixture. Cover with vinegar and oil and leave for at least 2-3 days before eating.

∽ 3 ∽

SOUPS
AND FIRST COURSES

*A soup does seven things: it relieves hunger
and quenches thirst, it fills the belly and
cleans the mouth, it eases slumber,
helps digest, and brings a flush to the cheeks.*

(*popular old verse*)

Tuscan bread is typically *sciocco*, or unsalted.
Housewives kneaded it for hours on end in the
madia (bread chest), and made the sign of the
cross on it to make it rise better, but also to bless
it, this fruit of the earth and hard labour. Once a
week, in turns, they took it to the local oven.
That bread lasted for days, and when it was dry it
was used for soups. This was an ancient custom.
At the end of medieval banquets, in fact, the
thick slices of bread used by guests to lay their
food on were gathered up and finished, together
with meat and vegetable leftovers, in the servants'
capacious cauldrons. Later, pasta or risotto
might be added, although true-born Florentines
continued to prefer bread or bean soups. Even
though the presence of broth ought really to
advise against wine, minestroni and soups
tolerate dry red wines well. The tomato in *pappa*
or on pasta, as also vegetable sauces, requires
light red or rosé wines. Fish sauces or dishes with
a strong taste of butter or milk must necessarily
be accompanied by dry white wine; for meat
sauces, instead, the wine should be red, young,
dry and light, becoming, in the case of game
sauces, more full-bodied and tannic.

Carabaccia

Onion soup

One kg of red onions; one stick of celery; one medium-sized carrot, diced; half a litre of broth*; 4 slices of toasted household bread*; 6 spoonfuls of extra virgin olive oil; plenty of grated Parmigiano; salt; pepper

Preparation: 30' - Cooking time: 1 h

Put the vegetables into an earthenware pan with the oil, the salt and the pepper. Cover and cook on a low flame for 30'. Add the broth and continue cooking for about 30'. In the meantime, toast the bread and arrange it in bowls; pour the soup over it, sprinkle with Parmigiano and serve.

In a version which is richer and more elaborately flavoured, the chopped mixture includes plenty of basil leaves, the broth is a chicken broth, and, after having bathed the onions in white wine, 100 g of seasonal legumes are added for every kg of onions. With just onions sautéed together with a couple of sausages and 50 g of bacon, the very tasty "cipollata" is made.

Minestra di fagioli

BEAN SOUP

🍲 200 g of short pasta; 500 g of fresh cannellini beans* (or 200 g if dry) boiled in half a litre of salt water; the water the beans are cooked in; 2 cloves of garlic; a small bunch of sage leaves; 6 spoonfuls of extra virgin olive oil

🍲 *Preparation: 5' - Cooking time: 30'*

🍲 Sauté the sage and garlic in 2 spoonfuls of oil. When the garlic starts to brown, remove it and pour into a casserole the beans that have been put through a mouli with their cooking water. When they start to boil add the pasta and continue cooking until obtaining the density desired. Add a dash of oil and serve.

🐟 *A tastier and more complex version involves combining with the bean liquid, before throwing in the pasta, lard, parsley and a pinch of chilli pepper, to be sautéed with the garlic before adding a large ripe tomato (or a spoonful of tomato sauce), salt and pepper. But you can also boil the beans with garlic and sage, put them through a mouli with their cooking water and blend with a fried mixture of garlic, rosemary and chilli pepper before throwing in the pasta. If the beans, boiled with water, oil, garlic and sage, are, with their broth, poured onto slices of toasted bread, this is the bastard or Lombard variety of the soup, whose name may derive from the Lombard merchant and artisan community once active in Florence outside Porta San Pietro, in the modern neighbourhood of Sant'Ambrogio.*

pignatta

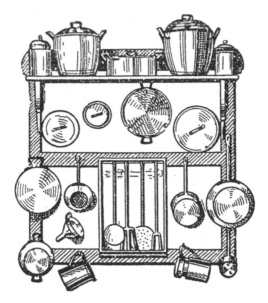

Pasta e ceci

PASTA AND CHICKPEAS

200 g of grooved short pasta; 200 g of soaked dried chickpeas*; one clove of garlic; a handful of rosemary leaves; 2 small ripe tomatoes, peeled and chopped; 2 litres of salt water; 3 spoonfuls of extra virgin olive oil; a pinch of pepper

Preparation: 5' - Cooking time: 2 h and 30'

On a low gas boil the chickpeas together with the oil, rosemary, garlic and tomatoes for at least 2 hours. Pass half through the mouli and combine with the cooking water together with the whole chickpeas; turn up the heat and throw in the pasta. When cooked, add the pepper, leave for a while and serve in bowls, dense and lukewarm. Garnish with a dash of oil.

To be tried with the addition of a few small squares of toasted bread rubbed with garlic.

Minestrone

FLORENTINE VEGETABLE SOUP

200 g of rice or short pasta; 250 g of fresh white beans* (or 100 g if dried), parboiled; 2 red onions with 2 carrots and 2 sticks of celery, finely chopped; 3 potatoes; 3 courgettes; 2 small ripe tomatoes, cut into small pieces; a bunch of chard with ¼ of a savoy cabbage cut into strips; a handful of chopped parsley; one litre of broth*; 6 spoonfuls of extra virgin olive oil; salt, pepper

Preparation: 30' - Cooking time: 1 h and 20'

Sauté the 'odori'* in the oil; when they start to brown combine with the other vegetables and the broth and cook with a lid on for an hour, stirring regularly. Taste for salt and pepper, throw in the pasta or rice and cook uncovered for another 15-20', adding more broth if necessary.

With rice this minestrone is better hot; with pasta it is also excellent cold, flavoured with a small handful of finely chopped basil; it can also be served with slices of toasted bread, either plain or rubbed with garlic.

Crespelle alla fiorentina
FLORENTINE-STYLE CREPES

A batter* prepared with: 100 g of '00' flour; 2 beaten eggs; one glass of milk; 50 g of melted butter; salt.
A filling made up of: 250 g of spinach, cleaned and washed; 200 g of fresh ricotta cheese; 2 spoonfuls of grated Parmigiano; one egg; a pinch of grated nutmeg; salt; pepper.
A condiment of: bechamel; 3 spoonfuls of tomato sauce; Parmigiano; a small knob of butter to grease the pan and the oven dish

Preparation: 20' in addition to the time for the batter to rest, and for the filling - *Cooking time:* 15' for the crepes, 15' for the filling and 20' for gratinating

For the batter mix the flour, eggs and salt; then add the milk and butter, a little at a time, and leave for 30'. In the meantime, cook the spinach, chop it up finely and blend together with all the other ingredients of the filling. Place a non-stick frying-pan on the gas, quickly melt a small knob of butter and fry the batter, making 8 crepes with it. Spread some filling onto each crepe, roll them up into small tubes and place them in a greased oven dish. Cover with bechamel, plenty of Parmigiano and blotches of tomato sauce, and gratinate in a moderate oven.

Maccheroni sul coniglio
Maccheroni with rabbit sauce

ↀ 400 g of maccheroni*; half a rabbit (with its liver), washed, dried and cut into pieces; a finely chopped mixture of: one onion, one carrot, one stick of celery, a small bunch of parsley, a sprig of rosemary, one clove of garlic, 50 g of bacon; 3 chopped ripe tomatoes, without skins or pips; half a glass of white wine; 6 spoonfuls of extra virgin olive oil; salt; pepper

ↀ *Preparation:* 40' - *Cooking time:* 1 h

ↀ Sauté the chopped vegetables, bacon and herbs in the oil; when they start to brown, add the rabbit and sauté well. Then add the tomatoes and chopped liver, salt, pepper and simmer* for about 30'. Remove the rabbit from the pan, separate the meat from the bone, cut into large pieces and put back in the sauce. Taste for salt and pepper and bathe in the wine over a high flame. As soon as it becomes dense, the sauce is ready. Pour it over the pasta and serve hot.

nauicella cō past
relle et 4 piedi

Pappardelle sull'anatra
PAPPARDELLE WITH DUCK SAUCE

ဗ 400 g of pappardelle*; half a small duck
(with its liver and heart), plucked, emptied,
washed, singed* and cut into pieces; 400 g
of ripe chopped tomatoes, without skins or pips;
a finely chopped mixture of: one onion, one
carrot, a stick of celery, 50 g of bacon; a glass of
white wine; 4 spoonfuls of extra virgin olive oil;
plenty of grated Parmigiano; salt; pepper

ဗ *Preparation:* 1 h - *Cooking time:* 1 h and 30'

ဗ Sauté the chopped vegetables and bacon
in oil; when soft, add the duck and sauté.
Bathe in the white wine. Add the tomatoes, salt
and pepper and simmer* for an hour.
Take the duck off the heat, skin it, remove
the bones, cut into large pieces and put in the
sauce with the chopped up liver and heart.
Adjust the seasoning and turn up the heat.
When it boils, the sauce is ready. Pour over the
pasta and serve with Parmigiano.

Penne strascicate

PASTA QUILLS SAUTÉED IN MEAT SAUCE

∽ 350 g of grooved pasta quills; 300 g of minced veal meat; 5 chopped ripe tomatoes, without skins or pips (or half a litre of tomato sauce); a finely chopped mixture of: one onion, one carrot, one stick of celery; one cup of broth*; 5 spoonfuls of extra virgin olive oil; salt; pepper

∽ *Preparation:* 15' - *Cooking time:* 1 h and 15'

∽ Sauté the chopped vegetables in the oil; when they start to soften, add the minced meat and cook for 30', stirring often and little by little adding the broth. Add the tomatoes and simmer* for at least an hour, stirring every now and then. In the meantime boil the pasta and when half cooked drain and pour together with the sauce into a casserole.
Cook on a low flame for about 10', sprinkling with Parmigiano just before removing from the heat.

∼ *If left over, the penne are excellent the following day, heated up again in the pan with the addition of a little water.*

45

Risotto coi carciofi

ARTICHOKE RISOTTO

300 g of Arborio or Ribe rice; 4 good-sized artichokes*, cleaned and cut into thin slices; 2 cloves of peeled garlic; a small bunch of parsley, chopped; 50 g of butter; half a glass of white wine; a litre of broth*; 50 g of grated Parmigiano; 4 spoonfuls of extra virgin olive oil; salt; pepper

Preparation: 15' - *Cooking time:* 35'

Sauté the whole cloves of garlic in the oil and half the butter; as soon as they brown, add the artichokes and sauté well, bathing in some of the broth. Add the rice and toast it on a medium flame, bathe in the wine and cook, stirring often and adding the hot broth little by little. When the cooking is over (after 20'), remove from the heat and blend in the rest of the butter and 2 spoonfuls of Parmigiano, stirring well. Serve hot and creamy, sprinkled with pepper and parsley and the leftover cheese.

The artichokes can be substituted with asparagus, peas or other vegetables "in bianco", i.e. without the addition of tomato.*

Risotto alla fiorentina
FLORENTINE-STYLE RISOTTO

300 g of Arborio or Ribe rice; 250 g of minced veal meat; a finely chopped mixture of: one onion, one carrot, one stick of celery, a small bunch of basil, a small bunch of parsley; a litre of broth*; 50 g of grated Parmigiano; 4 spoonfuls of extra virgin olive oil; salt; pepper

Preparation: 5' - *Cooking time:* 1 h

Gently sauté the chopped vegetables in the oil. Before they begin to soften, add the minced meat and cook on a medium heat for 30', stirring regularly. Then pour in the rice and complete the cooking, little by little bathing in the broth. Serve hot with a sprinkling of Parmigiano.

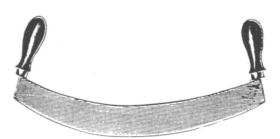

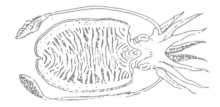

Risotto nero con le seppie alla fiorentina

FLORENTINE-STYLE BLACK RISOTTO
WITH CUTTLEFISH

⤺ 300 g of Arborio or Ribe rice; 400 g of cuttlefish*, well washed and with the little ink sacs cut into small pieces; 500 g of chard*, washed and cut into strips; one clove of garlic and half an onion, finely chopped; one spoonful of tomato sauce diluted in a little hot broth; a litre of broth*; one glass of white wine; 4 spoonfuls of extra virgin olive oil; salt; pepper

⤺ *Preparation: 30' - Cooking time: 30'*

⤺ Sauté the finely chopped garlic and onion in the oil; when browning, add the cuttlefish and the chard. After about 5', bathe in the wine and, when this has evaporated, pour in the rice and tomato sauce. Add salt and complete the cooking, adding the broth little by little and stirring regularly. A few minutes before taking off the heat, add the ink of the cuttlefish, sprinkle with pepper and serve hot.

&co 4 &co

MEAT CUTS, SCRAPS
AND OFFAL

*Florentines, we are all butchers
always looking for good meat
either for the love of it or for our earnings.*

(Ser Febo Prete, 16th C)

Meat has always been greatly appreciated in
Florence. Meat cut by the *beccai* – the butchers of
old – with an art that made the best use of the
various parts of the animal: choice cuts destined
for the aristocracy and the wealthy, and what was
left over for the less well-to-do, who resorted to
lengthy cooking and herbs to make the meat
more tender and more flavourful. Typical of the
Florentines is their predilection for offal, widespread among the people but also among the
higher ranks of society. The same goes for the
sausage, glorified as early as the Renaissance
because "it's good hot and cold and boiled and
burnt, before the meal and after, and in winter-
time it does more good than a hot fire and a fur
coat [...] and it's sold and cooked with laurel
because it's worthy of being crowned" (Matteo
Francesi, 16th C). Meats require red wine:
averagely full-bodied and aged for beef; smoother
and more robust for pork and rabbit; younger,
dry and sparkling for chicken, boiled meat and
fried meat; more mature for stews, more scented
and full-bodied for feathered game; aged,
harmonious and smooth for other game; lively
and dry for offal. With fricassee, however,
perfumed whites or reds are more suitable.

Agnello al forno
ROAST LAMB

℘ A leg of lamb with loin and **kidneys**;
2 cloves of chopped garlic; a handful of rosemary
leaves; half a glass of extra virgin olive oil; **salt**;
pepper

℘ *Preparation: 10' - Cooking time: 1 h*

℘ Rub the lamb well in the garlic, rosemary,
salt and pepper mixed together, grease it with
the oil and cook in a hot oven for at least an
hour, basting occasionally with the juices.
Halfway through the cooking, add potatoes cut
into pieces, turning regularly to season them.

Bistecca alla fiorentina
FLORENTINE-STYLE T-BONE STEAK

℘ A veal steak of the
Chianina variety, with
fillet and sirloin, not
less than 3 cm thick
but not thicker
than 4,5 cm; salt;
freshly ground
pepper

℘ *Preparation:*
the time needed to
prepare the charcoal and
heat the grid-iron -
Cooking time: 10-12'

℘ Lay the meat (not marinated* or soaked)
on a heated grid-iron placed about 10 cm above
live embers, without flames, and roast for 5-6'.
Turn it with a spatula, taking care not to pierce
the already cooked part; then roast the other
side. Salt at the end of the cooking and serve the
steak very hot and, if desired, with a sprinkling of
pepper.
The real "fiorentina" should be well roasted on
the outside, and pink and succulent though not
bloody on the inside.

℘ *It's difficult to say how many people can share a
juicy, well-roasted steak. Calculate its weight, therefore,
on the basis of people's appetite.*
*Ideal accompaniment: wild herb salad and boiled or
oven-stewed beans*.*

Stracotto alla fiorentina

FLORENTINE-STYLE BRAISED VEAL

୧⊘ 1.2 kg of veal, either sirloin or rump; 400 g of mashed ripe tomatoes; 80 g of lard or streaky bacon, in small pieces; 2 large whole carrots; one medium-sized onion with 2 carrots and 2 sticks of celery, thinly sliced; 2 glasses of red wine; one glass of broth*; 6 spoonfuls of extra virgin olive oil; salt; freshly ground pepper

୧⊘ *Preparation:* 20' in addition to the 10' for finishing - *Cooking time:* about 3 h

୧⊘ Make a hole in the meat that traverses its entire length and insert the carrots, one in each end, so that they meet in the middle, then lard* the meat with the fat, the salt and the pepper. In the meantime, cook the 'odori'* in the hot oil until they are soft, put the well-tied meat in and cook on a high flame for about 30', stirring well. Bathe in the wine, which should evaporate before adding the tomatoes. Salt, pepper, cover and cook for 2-3 hours, bathing with the broth if necessary and stirring often. When the meat is *stracotta* (literally overcooked), remove it, drain off the excess oil (which may be useful for other stews or sauces) and pass the residue through a sieve. Put everything back on the heat, stirring well for about 10', then untie the meat and cut it into slices, at the same time keeping the sauce warm. Lay the slices on a serving dish, pour over the sauce and serve.

୧⊷ *A perfect accompaniment is boiled or mashed potatoes, or even beans* "a guisa d'uccellini" (in the manner of small birds) – as Artusi calls them, who also recommends them with boiled meat* – though more commonly called "all'uccelletto" perhaps because of the sage which must always be used to cook small birds. The leftover sauce can be used with rice or pasta. Since, for the recipe to be successful, the piece of meat should not be of a weight less than that indicated, the doses are intended for 6 people.*

Polpettone di carne cruda alla fiorentina

FLORENTINE-STYLE MEATLOAF

ல௫ 500 g of minced veal; 80 g of finely chopped
cured ham, or mortadella, either on its own or
mixed with salame; 2 eggs; the soft part of a
bread roll soaked in milk and then wrung out;
60 g of grated Parmigiano; 500 g of chopped
ripe tomatoes, without skins or pips; a small
bunch of parsley; a finely chopped mixture of:
one small red onion, one stick of celery, one
carrot; one glass of red or white wine, according
to taste; flour or breadcrumbs; 6 spoonfuls of
extra virgin olive oil; salt; freshly ground pepper

ல௫ *Preparation:* 20' - *Cooking time:* 1 h and 30'

ல௫ Mix the meat together with the ham,
the eggs, the bread, the Parmigiano, the
softened bread, the parsley, the salt and the
pepper. As you sauté the 'odori'*, give the
mixture an elongated form and coat it either in
the flour or the breadcrumbs. Then sauté it in
the pan, making sure that it goldens all over.
Bathe in the wine and add the tomatoes.
Salt, pepper, cover and cook on a low flame
for about an hour. Serve the meatloaf in slices,
covered in its own sauce.

*This is the simplest ver-
sion, which can be enri-
ched in various ways.
For example, the
sauce can be
flavoured with a
fistful of dried
mushrooms soaked
in warm water, but
also with a grating
of nutmeg.
A summer version is cold
meatloaf, made by mixing the
meat with Parmigiano, eggs, nutmeg, chopped garlic and soft bread, boiled
and left to cool, and then, with all the 'odori', cooking
the well-tied mixture sewn in a gauze.
It should be served either with mayonnaise or with green
sauce, accompanied by pickles* or boiled vegetables.
A mini version of this meatloaf is 'meat rissoles', made
with the addition of garlic, parsley, Parmigiano, nutmeg and soft bread soaked in milk and wrung out,
coated in flour and fried.
The ideal accompaniment is boiled or reheated potatoes,
cardoons*, or other stewed vegetables.*

Arrosto morto

PAN-ROASTED VEAL

ജ 800 g of veal sir-
loin well tied so that it
keeps its shape; a finely
chopped mixture of:
one onion, one carrot,
one stick of celery, 2
bayleaves (garlic and
rosemary optional); a
glass of good red wine;
2 ladlefuls of broth*;
a dash of extra virgin
olive oil; salt; pepper

ജ *Preparation:* 15'
in addition to the
time needed to carve
the meat - *Cooking time:*
1 h and 15'

ജ Sauté the finely
chopped vegetables in
the oil, add the meat
and cook until golden on all sides over a high
flame. Salt, pepper and bathe in the wine. When
the wine has evaporated add the broth, lower the
heat and cook for about one hour and 30'. At
the end of the cooking the liquid will have been
consumed. Remove the meat from the pan, untie
it and serve it cut into slices with the sauce that is
left after cooking.

Braciole alla fiorentina

FLORENTINE-STYLE VEAL CUTLETS

ജ 600 g of veal slices, either topside or rump;
500 g of mashed ripe tomatoes; a finely chopped
mixture of: one small red onion, one stick of
celery, one medium-sized carrot; one glass of red
wine; 4 spoonfuls of extra virgin olive oil; salt;
pepper

ജ *Preparation:* 5', if the slices have already
been cut by the butcher - *Cooking time:* 1 h and 15'

ജ Sauté the finely chopped vegetables in
the oil and when they start to golden add the
meat slices and cook well on both sides. Bathe in
the wine and when this has evaporated add the
tomatoes, salt, pepper, cover and continue
cooking for about an hour on a very low flame,
adding a little water as necessary.

Arista

Roast loin of pork

෨ඁ 1.5 kg of loin of pork on the bone; 2 cloves of garlic chopped up with a small handful of rosemary leaves; a pinch of fennel seeds (optional); oil necessary for greasing an oven dish; salt; freshly ground black pepper

෨ඁ *Preparation:* 15' in addition to the time needed for deboning the meat - *Cooking time:* 2 h

෨ඁ Because of the tastiness of this roast, the ideal thing is to cook the meat without having deboned it previously. However, to carve it comfortably, an acceptable method is to detach it partially from the central bone and from the ribs with the help of a very sharp knife, inserting salt, pepper, garlic and rosemary between it and the flesh. Then make some incisions on the outside, fill them with the same seasoning, tie the meat well to the bone, spread the rest of the chopped herbs over it and cook in an oven preheated to 170 °C for at least 2 hours, basting regularly with the juices. At the end of the cooking, turn up the heat to turn golden.

෨ඁ *The juices obtained can be used not only to flavour the sliced meat, but also for cooking potatoes, to be added to the dish 30' before removing it from the heat, or for quickly sautéeing turnips and flowering turnip tops*, cabbage*, chard* and spinach.*

Cappone alla fiorentina
FLORENTINE-STYLE CAPON

⚬ A young capon weighing about 3 kg, cleaned and singed*; a finely chopped mixture of: one medium-sized red onion, one carrot, one stick of celery, one small clove of garlic, one bay-leaf, a pinch of thyme, fresh if possible (and, if desired, a small bunch of parsley); a good thick slice of cured ham cut into small strips; a small glass of Vinsanto; 2 glasses of tomato sauce; half a litre of broth*; 2 knobs of butter; 6 spoonfuls of extra virgin olive oil; salt; pepper

⚬ *Preparation:* 35' - *Cooking time:* 2 h and 30'

⚬ Tie the legs of the capon and sauté it well in oil and butter, on a moderate heat, together with the finely chopped vegetables, in such a way that it goldens all over. Turn down the heat and continue cooking for about 30', turning it often and basting it with its juices and with the broth. Add the ham and, when it has cooked, the tomato sauce. Taste for salt and pepper and continue, on a low flame, for another hour and 30'. Add the Vinsanto at the end of the cooking, allow it to evaporate, and serve the capon whole, accompanied by its own gravy. Alternatively the capon can be cut into pieces and garnished with slices of toasted bread soaked in the gravy which can be diluted with a little broth.

Stufato alla fiorentina
FLORENTINE-STYLE VEAL STEW

✿ 800 g of lean veal cut into large chunks;
400 g of skinned ripe tomatoes; 2 cloves of garlic;
a handful of rosemary leaves; a glass of red wine;
4 spoonfuls of extra virgin olive oil; salt; pepper

✿ *Preparation:* 5' - *Cooking time:* 1 h and 30'

✿ Sauté the meat well in the oil together with
the garlic and rosemary, turning it often, and
bathe in the wine. Add the tomatoes, salt,
pepper, and bring to the boil; then lower the
heat, cover and finish cooking, every now and
then stirring and adding a little water.

Variations of this stew depend on the 'odori'*
used (onion, carrot, celery and sage; onion, carrot,
celery, parsley, basil; onion, carrot, celery, garlic, basil;
garlic, chilli pepper and parsley) and the tomato (for
some, in fact, tinned tomato is a must – one spoonful,
diluted in a large cup of warm water). The meat can be
served either on its own or on slices of toasted bread,
rubbed with garlic as desired. You can also prepare it
by adding to the meat, during cooking, small chunks of
potatoes or peas.

Fagiano alla fiorentina
FLORENTINE-STYLE ROAST PHEASANT

✿ A pheasant weighing more than one kg;
150 g of chopped raw ham; 50 g of bacon cut
into thin slices; 4-5 sage leaves; half a glass of
white wine; vinegar; 4 spoonfuls of extra virgin
olive oil; salt; pepper

✿ *Preparation:* 1 h in addition to the time
needed for hanging the bird - *Cooking time:* 45'

✿ Hang the pheasant with its feathers for 3-4
days (though even more if it has been hunted);
empty it of its innards and pluck it carefully,
remove the feet and the head, singe* and wash
in water and vinegar.
Stuff it with the sage and the chopped peppered
ham and dress it with the slices of bacon. Tie
it up well and cook it in an oven pre-heated to
180 °C, bathing it in the wine and basting
with the juices. Untie it, remove the bacon and
serve in pieces together with the bacon and stuffing, steeped in the gravy made by the cooking.

Fegatelli di maiale
ROAST PIG'S LIVER

∽∾ 600 g of pig's liver cut into large pieces;
200 g of pig's omentum washed in warm water to
lay it out well and cut into squares; wooden
skewers, if possible of bay; bayleaves; some slices
of crostini* bread; extra virgin olive oil; salt;
pepper

∽∾ *Preparation:* 30' - *Cooking time:* 30'

∽∾ Wrap the pieces of liver in the omentum,
salt and pepper, and arrange on the skewers,
alternating them with bread slices and bayleaf
(although some prefer sage, as for small birds),
and cook them in a baking-pan, sprinkled with a
dash of oil, in a medium oven for about 30',
turning regularly. Even better, if you have one,
to roast them on a spit!

Fegato alla fiorentina
FLORENTINE-STYLE LIVER

ᴄ◉ 500 g of veal liver cut into thin slices; 5-6 sage leaves; 2 whole cloves of garlic; one cup of flour; 4 spoonfuls of extra virgin olive oil; salt; pepper

ᴄ◉ *Preparation: 10' - Cooking time: 15'*

ᴄ◉ Remove the hard parts of the slices of liver, wash them and dry them carefully. Sauté the garlic and sage in the oil, then lay the salted, peppered and lightly floured slices of liver in the pan. Cook for 10' on both sides and serve hot. But beware! As an old and very wise Tuscan saying goes, "Salt cod, liver and egg, the more they are boiled the harder they become".

Rognoni alla fiorentina
Florentine-style veal kidneys

🌀 2 veal kidneys; 100 g of butter; a small bunch of chopped parsley; breadcrumbs; half a glass of vinegar; salt; pepper

🌀 *Preparation:* 50' in addition to the time needed to leave the kidneys - *Cooking time:* about 30'

🌀 Cut the kidneys in half lengthways and carefully remove the fat. Soak them in cold water and vinegar for about 30', drain them and dry them well. Heat the butter and, when it begins to foam, put in the kidneys, salt, pepper and cook on a low flame for about 15'. Take off the heat, drain them well and roll them in breadcrumbs flavoured with salt, pepper and parsley. Leave them to rest for at least an hour, then roll them again in breadcrumbs and put them back on the heat for at least 10'. Serve hot

🐌 *An excellent alternative is kidney "trifolato", that is, sliced, coated in flour and sautéed in oil and butter on a high flame for a couple of minutes, stirring all the time. Add salt and, just before taking off the heat, a generous sprinkling of lemon juice and chopped parsley.*

Trippa alla fiorentina
FLORENTINE-STYLE TRIPE

🍲 One kg of tripe*, already cooked, washed and cut into strips 1 cm wide; 500 g of ripe tomatoes, skinned and cut into pieces; a finely chopped mixture of: one onion, one stick of celery, one carrot (or a small chopped onion); 3-4 spoonfuls of grated Parmigiano; 6 spoonfuls of extra virgin olive oil; salt; pepper

🍲 *Preparation:* 30' - *Cooking time:* 1 h

🍲 Sauté the chopped vegetables in the oil until soft, add the tripe and cook for about 15', stirring regularly, then add the tomatoes. Salt, pepper, and cook for about 30' on a moderate heat, until the cooking liquid has evaporated. Remove from the heat, sprinkle with Parmigiano and leave to rest for a few minutes.
Serve the tripe hot with more cheese. Ideal side dish: boiled or flask-cooked beans*.

🍥 *This is the authentic recipe for Florentine-style tripe, which is often confused with another, richer recipe that involves the addition of minced meat with the sautéed vegetables or even meat sauce diluted in a little water or broth*.*
Excellent sautéed in butter and oil with garlic and parsley and "finished off" with a delicious fricassee.*

5

SEAFOOD IN THE PAN

In March I can surely give you plenty of fish,
trout, eels, lamprey and salmon,
sea bream, dolphins and sturgeon,
and every other fish of our seas.

(Folgòre da San Gimignano, Sonnets, 16th C)

In Florence fish is synonymous, almost exclusively, with eels and salt cod, which are usually stewed but can also be roasted, and, until the middle of the 20th century, the small fried fish of the Arno river, which today, alas, have almost completely disappeared.

Snails can be stewed and frogs are fried; however, not only is it difficult to find them, these dishes also involve a long and laborious preparation. It is more advisable, therefore, to eat them in some specialized *trattoria* or, better still, hope that some more accomplished friend or lover of "humble" cuisine can prepare them for us. Cod, either dried (stockfish) or salted, came to Florence from Livorno with the cart or with the diligence. A dish served on Fridays, or in any case on "meatless" days, prepared with chickpeas, it was considered a poor food, but one that today has been revived by gourmets. Excellent with the unusual accompaniment of well-seasoned black-eyed beans. As for "baccalà alla fiorentina", a well-known diatribe exists with the Livornese, who claim this dish as their own. Wines for fish should be dry whites with medium structure; with fatty eels, stews and salt cod, young reds that are ready to drink are more suitable, or red wines of good balance and structure.

Anguilla alla fiorentina

FLORENTINE-STYLE EELS

One kg of eels*, cleaned, skinned and cut into sections about 6-7 cm long; 3 cloves of garlic cut into thin slices; 4-5 sage leaves; 200 g of breadcrumbs; one glass of red wine; a segment of lemon; half a glass of extra virgin olive oil; salt; pepper

Preparation: 20' in addition to the time necessary for the infusion - *Cooking time:* 50'

Soak the eel sections in an infusion with oil, salt and pepper for about one hour. Drain them, coat them in breadcrumbs and sauté in a pan in which you have fried the garlic and sage. Add the infusion liquid and put in a hot oven for about 40', basting occasionally with the wine and turning them over halfway through the cooking. Serve hot with a dash of lemon juice.

Anguilla al forno

BAKED EELS

One kg of eels*, cleaned, skinned and cut into sections about 6-7 cm long; 200 g of flour mixed with a handful of chopped rosemary leaves; a finely chopped mixture of: one red onion, one stick of celery, one carrot; a glass of red wine; 4 spoonfuls of extra virgin olive oil; salt

Preparation: 20' in addition to the time needed for the eels to rest - *Cooking time:* 25' in addition to the time for preparing the polenta

Sauté the chopped vegetables in an oven dish; when they start to brown, add the floured eel sections. Cook in a medium oven for 20', basting regularly with the wine. Salt, turn off the heat and leave for 15'; then remove from the oven and serve with corn-meal gnocchi*.

Baccalà lesso
BOILED SALT COD

இ 800 g of salt cod*, soaked and boned; one clove of garlic; a small bunch of parsley; 6-7 black peppercorns; half a glass of white wine; a segment of lemon; extra virgin olive oil

இ *Preparation:* 10' in addition to the time for leaving the fish - *Cooking time:* 15'

இ Put the fish into a casserole just covered with cold water together with the 'odori'*, the pepper and the wine. Simmer* for 10', then turn off the heat and leave for 5'. Drain and season with oil, pepper and lemon.

Excellent drained, as soon as the water boils, dried and fried in a light batter of flour, water, white wine and chopped parsley, garnished with more parsley and lemon. Ideal accompaniment, black-eyed beans* with a dressing of oil, salt and a drop of vinegar.*

Baccalà con i ceci
SALT COD WITH CHICKPEAS

இ 600 g of salt cod*, soaked and boned; 400 g of boiled chickpeas*; the liquid of the cooked chickpeas; 800 g of chard*, boiled and cut; 3 leeks, finely sliced; 6 spoonfuls of extra virgin olive oil; salt; pepper

இ *Preparation:* 30' - *Cooking time:* 45'

இ Sauté the leeks in an oven dish with the oil; when they start to brown add the fish cut into pieces and fry on both sides over a high flame. Remove, drain and lay on a piece of kitchen paper to dry. In the meantime, mix the chard in with the cooked leeks, add the chickpeas with some of their broth; adjust the salt, pepper and lay in the fish. Gratinate for 20' in a hot oven.

Excellent also with the chickpeas simply boiled, the fish takes on unexpected flavour filtering over the cooked legumes the oil in which you will have sautéed garlic, sage, bayleaf and rosemary and replacing the chard with spinach.

Baccalà alla fiorentina
FLORENTINE-STYLE SALT COD

🍃 800 g of salt cod*, soaked, boned and cut into pieces; 400 g of ripe tomatoes in pieces, without skins or pips; 2 cloves of peeled garlic; 2 finely sliced leeks; 6 spoonfuls of flour; one spoonful of chopped parsley; 4 spoonfuls of extra virgin olive oil; plenty of frying oil; salt; pepper

🍃 *Preparation:* 20' - *Cooking time:* 25'

🍃 Sauté the leeks and garlic in the oil. As soon as they start to brown add the tomatoes, salt, pepper and simmer* for 15'. Meanwhile, coat the fish with the flour and fry it in the oil on a medium heat on both sides. Drain it, dry it on kitchen paper and then cook it in the sauce for 5' on a low flame. Serve with a sprinkling of parsley.

🍃 *For an even richer taste, add a sliced red onion to the sauté mixture, or garlic and rosemary to the frying oil. If there are any leftovers you can prepare a tasty spaghetti sauce by breaking up the fish with a fork and adding a couple of chilli peppers.*

Frittelle di baccalà
SALT COD FRITTERS

🍃 400 g of salt cod*, soaked and boned; a batter* prepared with: 150 g of flour; half a small cup of milk and half of wine; 2 spoonfuls of extra virgin olive oil; one teaspoon of pizza yeast; plenty of frying oil; salt; pepper

🍃 *Preparation:* 20' in addition to the time needed for leaving the mixture - *Cooking time:* 15'

🍃 Break the fish up with a fork and mix the pieces in with the batter.
Leave for a couple of hours in a cool place or in the refrigerator, mix again and then fry in spoonfuls in hot oil.
Golden the fritters on both sides, remove, drain and dry on kitchen paper.
Serve hot and crispy, accompanied by vegetables sautéed in garlic and oil.

Seppie in zimino
STEWED CUTTLEFISH WITH CHARD

✑ 800 g of cuttlefish*, cleaned, cut into slices and washed; 800 g of chard* leaves (or spinach), boiled, squeezed and coarsely chopped; a finely chopped mixture of: one red onion, one carrot, one stick of celery, 2 cloves of garlic, a bunch of parsley; one glass of white wine; 6 spoonfuls of extra virgin olive oil; salt; freshly ground pepper

✑ *Preparation:* 20' - *Cooking time:* 40'

✑ Sauté the finely chopped vegetables in a pot, possibly of earthenware. As soon as they start to turn colour, add the cuttlefish and cook for 10'. Bathe in the wine; then mix in the vegetables, salt, pepper and continue to cook for 20', adding a little hot water if necessary. Turn off the heat, leave for a few minutes and serve with a sprinkling of more pepper

🍴 *Squid, which some prefer for the making of this dish (perhaps with an onion only), are perhaps more tender and delicate; but whatever one's tastes, this is a "classic" dish conceived for cuttlefish and salt cod*. To prevent the cuttlefish from becoming hard even at the end of the cooking, put a cork top in their sauce: a simple little precaution, but highly effective.*

Calamari con i piselli
SQUID WITH PEAS

✑ One kg of squid*, cleaned, cut into strips and rinsed in water; 250 g of freshly shelled peas; 2 ripe tomatoes in pieces, without skins or pips; a glass of weak broth*; a finely chopped mixture of: half an onion, one clove of garlic and a bunch of parsley; 4 spoonfuls of extra virgin olive oil; salt; pepper

✑ *Preparation:* 45' - *Cooking time:* 40'

✑ Sauté the finely chopped herb mixture in the oil; when it starts to brown, stir in the squid so that it absorbs the flavour. Salt, pepper, pour over the broth, add the tomatoes and simmer* for 10'. Add the peas and complete the cooking (about 20').

🍴 *Cuttlefish are, of course, also suitable for the preparation of this dish.*

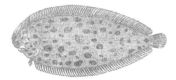

Sogliole alla fiorentina
FLORENTINE-STYLE SOLE

ↄ◯ 8 floured fillets of sole; 800 g of spinach, boiled, squeezed and roughly chopped; a bechamel sauce made with: 30 g of butter; 50 g of flour; half a litre of milk; one glass of white wine; 3 spoonfuls of grated Parmigiano; 70 g of butter; extra virgin olive oil; salt; pepper

ↄ◯ *Preparation:* 30' - *Cooking time:* 1 h and 20'

ↄ◯ While you sauté the spinach in a pan with half the butter, sauté the sole in another pan with the other half; bathe in the wine, salt and pepper. With the remaining butter grease an oven-dish and lay the spinach in with the sole on top. Cover with bechamel sauce mixed with any bits that are left in the fish pan, sprinkle with Parmigiano and gratinate for 20' in a hot oven.

Trote gratinate
BAKED TROUT

ↄ◯ 4 trout weighing about 250 g each, scraped, gutted, washed and dried; 200 g of grated Gruyère cheese; 80 g of butter; 2 egg yolks beaten with 3 spoonfuls of milk and a pinch of salt; one spoonful of chopped parsley; one teaspoon of thyme; 2 spoonfuls of breadcrumbs; salt; pepper

ↄ◯ *Preparation:* 45' - *Cooking time:* 35'

ↄ◯ Put the butter and aromatic herbs in a pot, ideally made of earthenware, and sauté the trout well on both sides, turning delicately. When a kind of crust has formed, add the eggs and cook for a few minutes on a low flame. Sprinkle with the Gruyère, the breadcrumbs and the pepper and gratinate in a hot oven for 20'.

❧ 6 ❧

IN FIELD AND GARDEN

Come to the door, my fair lady
For I have brought you a basket of salad.
I have brought you every kind of fine herb
(come to the door, my lady queen)
chickling, endive, 'metaschio' and rocket,
mint, 'fiorranza', calamint and borage.

(Anonymous, 13th C)

The land around Florence is a land of farmers and vine-growers. In Florence vegetables are eaten raw, in salads or in *pinzimonio* (dipped in oil and salt), and are cooked in a thousand different ways, all of them tasty and wholesome: simply boiled with a dash of the purest cold-pressed mill oil, *pizzichino* (pungent) when new, or sometimes with a drop of vinegar; or in soups, in the pot, in the oven, in an omelette, in tomato sauce, in a pie, fried. And in addition to what you can find at the market, there are others that grow along riverbanks or hedgerows, – like wild clematis shoots that sprout in spring – or in fields, like nettle, mallow and watercress...
Legumes are also much-loved, boiled lovingly and seasoned with that indispensable dash of oil and a few drops of vinegar. And scented herbs, the *odori*, which are added to dishes to enrapture the smell even before they reach the palate.
If they are not served as a side dish, in which case they are eaten with the same wine accompanying the main course, vegetables – with the exception of artichokes – require young dry whites of medium structure; for legumes, instead, medium-bodied young reds are the order of the day.

Asparagi alla fiorentina
FLORENTINE-STYLE ASPARAGUS

ᘒ One kg of large asparagus* shoots; 4 fresh eggs; 80 g of butter; 40 g of grated Parmigiano; salt; freshly ground black pepper

ᘒ *Preparation: 20' - Cooking time: 25'* in addition to the time for frying the eggs

ᘒ Cook the asparagus on a moderate heat in 50 g of butter for 5', stirring and turning gently. Before removing from the heat, sprinkle with Parmigiano and pepper. Serve them in a hot serving dish, dressed with their own sauce and garnished with the eggs which can be fried in the pan in the remaining butter.

Baccelli stufati
STEWED BROAD BEANS

ᘒ 2 kg of fresh, shelled broad beans*; one small onion, chopped; 4 ripe tomatoes cut into pieces, without skins or pips; one cup of broth*; a small bunch of fresh basil leaves; 4 spoonfuls of extra virgin olive oil; salt; pepper

ᘒ *Preparation: 25' - Cooking time: 35'*

ᘒ Cook the onion in the oil until it is soft, then add the broad beans, the tomatoes and the basil. Salt, pepper and cook for 30' with the lid on, stirring occasionally and adding broth if necessary.

ᘒ *An excellent variation uses a finely chopped mixture of onion and bacon (or ham) and a glass of white wine as an alternative to the broth.*

Carciofi alla fiorentina
FLORENTINE-STYLE ARTICHOKES

✍ 8 large artichokes* (*mamme*), cleaned, cut flat on the bottom and hollowed out in the middle; 200 g of cooked spinach, squeezed and chopped; 50 g of butter; 4 spoonfuls of cream; half a litre of bechamel sauce; one lemon; 4 spoonfuls of grated Parmigiano; salt; pepper

✍ *Preparation:* 30' - *Cooking time:* 1 h

✍ Boil the artichokes in salt water for 5', drain them and cook them quickly in a pan with cream, butter and salt. Then arrange them in an oven dish, fill them with the spinach mixed with what may be left in the pan, cover them with bechamel sauce and gratinate in a hot oven for 20' with a sprinkling of Parmigiano.

Carciofi ritti al forno e in tegame
BAKED UPRIGHT ARTICHOKES

✍ 8 large artichokes* (*mamme*), cleaned, cut flat on the bottom and with their stems well peeled; a finely chopped mixture of: 2 cloves of garlic, a small bunch of parsley, 100 g of bacon, some artichoke stems, half a glass of water; 4 spoonfuls of extra virgin olive oil, salt; pepper

✍ *Preparation:* 30' - *Cooking time:* 40'

✍ Arrange the artichokes upright in an oven-dish with the leaves splayed, filling the spaces between them with the finely chopped mixture, salt and pepper. Add the stems, bathe in water and oil and cook in a moderate oven, bathing them every now and then in their own sauce.

✍ *These artichokes can also be cooked in a pan with a finely chopped mixture of garlic, thyme and parsley or sprinkled with calamint and parsley.*

69

Cavolo strascicato
CASSEROLED CAULIFLOWER

✑ One cauliflower* weighing about one kg, stripped of its hard leaves; 300 g of ripe tomatoes cut into pieces, without skins or pips; 100 g of stoned black olives, chopped; 3 cloves of garlic; 4 spoonfuls of extra virgin olive oil; salt; pepper

✑ *Preparation:* 15' in addition to the time for leaving the cauliflower to cool - *Cooking time:* 25'

✑ Boil the cauliflower for 10', drain it and, when just warm, break up into florets and chop the core into small pieces. In the meantime, sauté the garlic in the oil, stir in the cauliflower, add the olives and tomatoes, salt, pepper and put in a medium oven or on the heat for 10'.

✑ *A simpler version involves sautéing the cauli in the pan with garlic and oil only; a richer version involves frying sausage, onion and parsley or thyme.*

Patate rifatte
TWICE-COOKED POTATOES

✑ 800 g of peeled potatoes cut into large pieces; 400 g of ripe chopped tomatoes, without skins or pips (or half a litre of tomato sauce); 2 whole cloves of garlic; a small bunch of sage; 5 spoonfuls of extra virgin olive oil; salt; pepper

✑ *Preparation:* 20' - *Cooking time:* 30'

✑ Sauté the garlic and sage in the oil. Before they start to brown, add the potatoes and stir in the oil on a high heat. Add the tomatoes, salt, pepper and cook on a low flame for about 20', occasionally adding a little water.

✑ *Excellent as a side dish for roast or boiled meat*, they are particularly recommended for "reheating" leftover boiled meat, which should be added to the potatoes together with the tomatoes.*

Fagioli all'uccelletto

BEANS IN TOMATO SAUCE

🌀 400 g of dry cannellini beans* (or one kg if fresh), boiled; 300 g of ripe tomatoes cut into pieces, without skins or pips; 3 cloves of unpeeled garlic; a bunch of sage leaves; 6 spoonfuls of extra virgin olive oil; salt; pepper

🌀 *Preparation:* 10' - *Cooking time:* 30'

🌀 Sauté the garlic and sage in the oil, add the tomatoes and cook for 15'. Stir in the boiled beans together with some of their liquid, taste for salt and pepper and simmer* for another 15'.

Cipolle al forno

BAKED ONIONS

🌀 4 large peeled red onions; one spoonful of chopped parsley; 4 spoonfuls of extra virgin olive oil; a dash of vinegar; salt; pepper

🌀 *Preparation:* 20' - *Cooking time:* 30'

🌀 Parboil the onions in salt water for about 15'. Flatten the tops and bottoms with a knife, cut in half horizontally and slightly hollow out the middles with a teaspoon. Arrange them in a pan and season with parsley, salt and pepper. Pour on a dash of oil and cook in a moderate oven for 15', bathing frequently with the juices. Serve with a dash of vinegar.

🦢 *Also excellent are stuffed onions, filled with a little onion chopped up with mortadella, cooked chard* and a boiled egg mixed with 2 spoonfuls of bread-crumbs and Parmigiano.*

Piselli alla fiorentina
FLORENTINE-STYLE PEAS

✑ 500 g of shelled peas (weighing 1,200 kg with the pods); 100 g of diced bacon; 3 cloves of unpeeled garlic (or one small fresh garlic); a small bunch of parsley; one teaspoon of sugar; 6 spoonfuls of extra virgin olive oil; salt; pepper

✑ *Preparation:* 5' in addition to the time needed to shell the peas - *Cooking time:* 30'

✑ Put the peas in a pan with oil, garlic and parsley, just cover them with cold water, salt and cook on a moderate heat.
Just before taking them off the heat add the bacon and the sugar. Taste for salt and pepper and serve.

🖎 *A very pleasant variation is peas with ham, which is prepared by mixing the peas with fried spring onion and ham and simmering them with chopped parsley, sugar and very little broth*.*

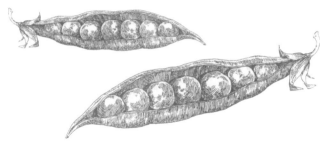

Fagiolini alla fiorentina
FLORENTINE-STYLE GREEN BEANS

✑ 800 g of French beans, topped and tailed and with any stringiness removed, washed and drained; 4 ripe tomatoes cut into pieces, without skins or pips; one finely sliced red onion; one carrot, diced; 5 spoonfuls of extra virgin olive oil; salt; pepper

✑ *Preparation:* 30' - *Cooking time:* 1 h

✑ Sauté the onion and carrot in the oil, add the beans, cover and cook for 10' on a low flame, stirring frequently. Add the tomatoes, salt and pepper and simmer* for 40'.

🖎 *A delicious variation of these stewed beans involves adding 2 unpeeled cloves of garlic to the initial sauté ingredients and a small bunch of basil leaves to the tomato.*

Gobbi trippati

CARDOONS COOKED LIKE TRIPE

🌀 800 g of small or medium cardoons (*gobbi*); 100 g of butter; 100 g of flour; 2 cloves of garlic cut in half (or a finely sliced white onion); one lemon; 100 g of grated Parmigiano; salt

🌀 *Preparation:* 25' in addition to the time for cooling the cardoons - *Cooking time:* 1 h and 15'

🌀 Clean the cardoons, cut them into pieces 6-7 cm long and simmer* for about an hour. Drain them and while they cool sauté the garlic in butter. Add the flour-dusted cardoons, cook on a low flame for about ten minutes and serve hot with a sprinkling of Parmigiano.

🌀 *Gratinating them quickly in the oven is optional. Adding tomato and basil instead of Parmigiano makes a very tasty stew. However, after having boiled them, you can also coat them in egg and then flour and fry them in plenty of oil; if they get left over, they are excellent cooked up again with tomato.*

Rapini saltati

SAUTÉED TURNIP GREENS

🌀 700 g of thoroughly washed turnip leaves*; 2 cloves of garlic cut into slices; 6 spoonfuls of extra virgin olive oil; salt; pepper

🌀 *Preparation:* 20' in addition to the time needed to cool the turnip leaves - *Cooking time:* 50'

🌀 Boil the turnip leaves in salt water for about 30'. Drain them, leave them to cool, and squeeze out as much water as possible. Sauté the garlic in the oil and when it starts to brown add the chopped turnip leaves. Salt, pepper and cook on a high flame for about 15', stirring regularly.

Spinaci alla fiorentina
FLORENTINE-STYLE SPINACH

One kg of fresh spinach; 50 g of butter; 4 eggs; 2 whole cloves of garlic; half a litre of bechamel sauce; grated Parmigiano; extra virgin olive oil; salt; pepper

Preparation: 20' in addition to the time for cooling the spinach - *Cooking time:* 1 h and 10'

Cook the spinach, let cool and squeeze out as much water as possible. Sauté the garlic in the oil and when it starts to brown add the chopped up spinach. Salt and stir on a high flame for about 10'. Add half of the bechamel and pour the mixture into a greased oven dish, making 4 little hollows in it. Into each hollow crack a whole egg and sprinkle with salt and pepper. Cover with the rest of the bechamel sauce and gratinate in a hot oven for about 20'.

With a few drops of lemon juice, boiled spinach sautéed in garlic and oil makes an excellent side dish for either boiled or roast meat.

Zucchini al tegame
SAUTÉED COURGETTES

500 g of courgettes, cleaned, cut into pieces or into fairly thick slices; 3 ripe tomatoes cut into pieces, without skins or pips; one small red onion, finely sliced; a small bunch of basil; 6 spoonfuls of extra virgin olive oil; salt; pepper

Preparation: 15' - *Cooking time:* 30'

Put all the ingredients into a casserole. Cover and bring to the boil on a low heat. Taste for salt and pepper and serve.

This simple dish, which goes well with boiled meat*, can be served with grated pecorino cheese. "Zucchini al funghetto", with or without tomatoes, can be seasoned instead with garlic and parsley, though you can also try with mint, calamint, marjoram…

∞ 7 ∞

EGGS, OMELETTES AND SAVOURY PIES

And now, how shall I cook it? Shall I make an omelette?… No, it would be better to cook it in a pannikin!… Or would it not be more savoury to fry it in the frying-pan? Or shall I simply boil it? No, the quickest way of all is to cook it in a pannikin: I am in such a hurry to eat it!

(Carlo Collodi, The Adventures of Pinocchio, *1883)*

An egg fried in the pan with the white firmly set and the yoke cooked but still soft, an omelette cooked on both sides, a plump pie, these are very simple dishes which are deceptively easy to make. Lightly heat the white of an egg in a small knob of butter or in some hot oil, add a little salt, then place the yoke in the middle of it with a sprinkling of pepper and on a very low flame cook your perfect pan-fried egg. A golden round omelette, whether simple or elaborate, when folded onto itself resembles what in Renaissance Florence was called *pesceduovo* (eggfish), because of its shape. Pies are cooked in the oven: a hot oven if you like a golden crust, a low oven if you like it creamy. Lastly, how to effortlessly peel the shell off a hard-boiled egg: cool it down under cold water, make a crack along its length, blow into it and *voilà*, it's done. Dry, delicate, white wines are the most suitable accompaniment, although with very tasty ingredients a rosé or light red wine is also acceptable. Artichoke pies are best eaten with water alone.

Uova al pomodoro
EGG AND TOMATOES

🍥 4 eggs; 2 ripe tomatoes cut into pieces, without skins or pips; 2 spoonfuls of extra virgin olive oil; salt; pepper

🍥 *Preparation:* 10' - *Cooking time:* 15'

🍥 Sauté the tomatoes in the oil for 10'. Salt, pepper and add the eggs, stirring the whites in gently without breaking the yokes, which should remain intact. Cook until the whites have set and serve on slices of toasted bread.

🐚 *Another tasty version uses tomatoes that are not too ripe and unpeeled cloves of garlic which can be removed before adding the eggs.*

Uova ripiene
STUFFED EGGS

🍥 4 hard-boiled eggs, peeled and cut into halves; 2 generous spoonfuls of anchovy sauce, better without garlic; salt; pepper

🍥 *Preparation:* 15' in addition to the time needed to cool the mixture - *Cooking time:* 15'

🍥 Take the yokes, mash them well and mix together with the anchovy sauce. Salt, pepper, and fill the half whites with the mixture. Leave in a cool place for a couple of hours and serve.

Frittata con gli asparagi
ASPARAGUS OMELETTE

ↂ A bunch of wild asparagus*, boiled and with the hard parts removed; 4 eggs beaten with a little salt and pepper; 50 g of butter

ↂ *Preparation: 5' - Cooking time: 15'*

ↂ Sauté the asparagus tips in the butter over a low flame. Turn up the heat and, when the butter fries, mix in the eggs. Lower the heat again and allow the eggs to set by covering or turning the omelette half way through the cooking.

Frittata con il cavolfiore
CAULIFLOWER OMELETTE

ↂ Half a cauliflower* with the hard leaves and core removed, broken up into florets; 3 cloves of chopped garlic; 3 eggs beaten with a pinch of salt; 2 spoonfuls of water; 2 spoonfuls of extra virgin olive oil; salt; pepper

ↂ *Preparation: 10' - Cooking time: 45'*

ↂ Sauté the garlic and cauliflower over a low flame. Add the water, salt, pepper and cook without turning up the heat for about 20'. When the cauli is cooked, add the eggs and allow to set, turning the omelette half way through cooking.

Frittata di cipolle

ONION OMELETTE

✑ 6 red onions cut into thin slices; 4 eggs beaten with a little salt and pepper; 2 spoonfuls of extra virgin olive oil; salt

✑ *Preparation: 15' - Cooking time: 20'*

✑ Fry the onions in the oil, salt lightly and add the eggs, lowering the heat. Allow the eggs to set and turn the omelette half way through the cooking.

Excellent also with well peeled leeks cooked on a low flame with oil and salt before adding the beaten eggs.

Frittata verde

GREEN OMELETTE

✑ 4 eggs beaten with a little salt; 400 g of vegetables, boiled, squeezed and finely chopped (spinach, nettles or other green leafy vegetables); 2 spoonfuls of extra virgin olive oil; salt

✑ *Preparation: 15' - Cooking time: 15'*

✑ Sauté the spinach in the oil. When it is completely dry, salt lightly and add the eggs. Cover and allow the egg mixture to set on a low flame.

Frittata con i gobbi
CARDOON OMELETTE

🍃 500 g of small or medium-sized cardoons*; 4 eggs beaten with a little salt; 80 g of flour; 8 spoonfuls of extra virgin olive oil

🍃 *Preparation: 20' - Cooking time: 1 h and 30'*

🍃 Clean the cardoons, cut them into pieces about 6-7 cm long and simmer* for about an hour. Drain them, leave them to cool, coat them in flour and sauté them in the oil. Add the eggs and allow to set, turning the omelette halfway through the cooking.

padella p̄ fare oui frittolate

Frittata con le patate
POTATO OMELETTE

🍃 500 g of potatoes; 4 eggs beaten with a little salt and pepper; 50 g of flour; 8 spoonfuls of extra virgin olive oil; salt; pepper

🍃 *Preparation: 20' - Cooking time: 30'*

🍃 Cut the potatoes into round slices, coat them in flour and fry on a low flame, turning them one by one. Add the eggs, allow them to set and turn the omelette halfway through the cooking.

🍃 *With the same method you can make an excellent omelette with courgettes (you will need at least 4), better still if flavoured with a few leaves of marjoram or fresh mint. Or with mushrooms, washing the caps well and seasoning with garlic, salt and pepper.*

79

Frittata con gli zoccoli
BACON OMELETTE

🍲 200 g of diced bacon; 4 eggs beaten with a little salt and pepper; 2 spoonfuls of extra virgin olive oil

🍲 *Preparation:* 10' - *Cooking time:* 15'

🍲 Sauté the bacon in the oil. As soon as it starts to brown add the eggs and allow them to set on a low flame, turning the omelette halfway through the cooking. Serve hot.

🍲 *This old recipe, which can also be done with ham, has a creamier version: just cook the omelette with a lid, without turning. Artusi, instead, advises folding it in half. Another tasty version uses sausage, which must be peeled and the meat crumbled; in both cases be careful with the salt!*

Frittatine trippate
EGG OMELETTES
WITH TOMATO SAUCE

🍲 6 eggs beaten with ¼ a glass of milk and a little salt; 300 g of chopped tomatoes, without skins or pips; 50 g of grated Parmigiano; 6 spoonfuls of extra virgin olive oil; salt; pepper

🍲 *Preparation:* 30' - *Cooking time:* 1 h

🍲 Make little omelettes by pouring the beaten eggs into the oil a little at a time. Roll them up and cut into slices. Prepare a sauce by cooking the tomatoes for about 30' in hot oil with salt and pepper. Lay in the small omelettes, cook them on a low heat for 15' and serve with a sprinkling of Parmigiano.

Tortino di pomodori
GREEN TOMATO PIE

ᘓᘖ 3 still green or just pinkish salad tomatoes, cut into horizontal slices and with the pips removed; 4 eggs beaten with a little salt; 50 g of flour; salt; plenty of frying oil

ᘓᘖ *Preparation:* 10' - *Cooking time:* 20'

ᘓᘖ Coat the tomato slices in flour and fry them on both sides in hot oil. Salt them and lay them in an oil-greased oven dish, add the eggs and cook in a hot oven for about 10'.

Tortino di carciofi
ARTICHOKE PIE

ᘓᘖ 6 small, tender artichokes*, well washed; 5 eggs beaten with a little salt; one clove of garlic; a small bunch of chopped parsley; 50 g of flour; 8 spoonfuls of extra virgin olive oil; salt; pepper

ᘓᘖ *Preparation:* 15' - *Cooking time:* 20'

ᘓᘖ Cut the artichokes into slices, not too thin, lightly coat them in flour and sauté in a pan with the oil and garlic. Salt, pepper and, when cooked, remove the garlic and sprinkle with parsley. Arrange them in an oven dish, pour the cooking sauce over them, add the eggs and put them in a hot oven. This dish is excellent whether creamy or completely set. A dash of lemon juice gives it an extremely refreshing taste.

Tortino di patate
POTATO PIE

◯ 400 g of potatoes, boiled, peeled and cut into thick slices; 2 eggs beaten with a little salt; 100 g of butter; 50 g of grated Parmigiano; a small bunch of chopped parsley; ¼ a litre of bechamel sauce; breadcrumbs; salt; pepper

◯ *Preparation:* 30' - *Cooking time:* 1 h

◯ Sauté the potatoes in half the butter, salt them, pepper them and arrange them in a greased oven dish coated in breadcrumbs. Prepare the bechamel sauce, allow it to cool, mix it with the eggs and parsley and pour it over the potatoes. Sprinkle with breadcrumbs and flecks of butter and grill in a hot oven until a golden crust forms.

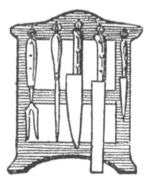

Tortino di uova
EGG PIE

◯ 6 eggs; 4 spoonfuls of cream; 50 g of butter; 4 slices of toasted household bread; salt; freshly ground pepper

◯ *Preparation:* 5' - *Cooking time:* 10'

◯ Beat the eggs directly in a pan, together with the cream and the salt, add the butter and cook for a few minutes on a very low flame, stirring continuously. When creamy, sprinkle with pepper and serve on slices of bread.

8

SEASONINGS
AND FLAVOURINGS

For festive occasions my art is always the same
I sit in the kitchen and to the song of a girl
I pound the mortar until the sauce is made.

(Antonio Cammelli, late 15th C)

Florentine cuisine contains sour flavours and seasonings directly inherited from the Middle Ages, based on wine, vinegar, sour grape juice or broth, as well as thick sauces mixed with oil, eggs and butter, taken from the aristocratic and royal cuisine of France between the 17th and 18th century. The great virtues of sour grape juice had always been lauded by popular tradition: it soothed pains, prevented infection, kindled passions and alleviated the suffering of childbirth. As for mustard, its very name, *mosto ardente*, derived from its being made from grape must and hot white mustard. Then there was *salsa verde*, perfect with boiled meat, sauces based on pepper, walnuts, almonds and pine-nuts, and the more recent sauces made with bell-pepper and tomato from the New World. In the Middle Ages sauces were sold ready-made by *speziali*, together with confectionery, sugar, medications and, of course, spices. Later they were supplied by itinerant pedlars, usually from the countryside, who would gather fresh, aromatic herbs and blend them with a wisdom dictated by experience and tradition. Today we can prepare them in the home and discover just how different they are from those that are sold in the shops.

Agresto
SOUR GRAPE SAUCE

ᴇᴐ The juice of 10-12 bunches of grapes;
2 glasses of good white wine vinegar

ᴇᴐ *Preparation: 15' - Cooking time: 40'*

ᴇᴐ Bring the vinegar and grape juice to the
boil; cook for 30' on a low heat, remove the
froth, filter and bottle in an air-tight container.

ᶓ☛ *By adding different aromas to the liquid you will
obtain a great variety of flavours. Here are some:*
*- for fried courgettes: mint, parsley, basil, fresh wild
fennel*
*- for poultry, game and meat: a small spoonful of finely
chopped onion and an orange peel. Bottle and cover
with oil*
*- a handful of basil leaves, 20 peeled fresh walnuts, a
fistful of the soft part of bread*
*- peeled fresh walnuts, the soft part of bread, a
bunch of parsley, half an onion, one clove of garlic,
one teaspoon of sugar, and perhaps half a spring
onion; pass through a mouli, heat, bottle and cover
with oil.*

Mostarda toscana
TUSCAN MUSTARD

ᴇᴐ 2 kg of red or white grapes (preferably
Canaiolo); one kg of red apples and 2-3 good
pears cut into slices; one glass of Vinsanto;
2 spoonfuls of honey; 50 g of mustard powder
mixed with a little Vinsanto; 50 g of candied
citron-peel and 50 g of candied orange-peel,
diced; one glass of good wine vinegar; salt

ᴇᴐ *Preparation: 30' in addition to the time for
macerating the grapes and cooling the sauce -
Cooking time: 30'*

ᴇᴐ Crush the grapes and leave to macerate in
a terrine for a couple of days. Then press them
and filter their juice. Meanwhile, simmer* the
fruit in the Vinsanto until it has evaporated; add
the grape juice, the honey, a pinch of salt and
cook again for 15' on a low flame until a dense
jam forms. Remove from the heat; add the
mustard, the vinegar and the candied peel and
cool. Bottle in air-tight jars.

ᶓ☛ *A sauce that was once made with must. Excellent
with roasts, it is an ideal accompaniment to boiled meat*.*

84

Salsa di noci
WALNUT SAUCE

One kg of fresh walnuts (or dry ones, though the taste will be different), shelled and peeled; a bunch of parsley leaves; one spoonful of capers; one glass of extra virgin olive oil; 2-3 spoonfuls of vinegar; salt; pepper

Preparation: 1 h

Chop and blend the walnuts together with the capers and the parsley and whip the mixture, pouring in the oil a drop at a time, then the salt, pepper and vinegar, stirring continuously.

Excellent with boiled meat* and with roasts.

Acciugata
ANCHOVY SAUCE

4 salted anchovies (desalted and carefully filleted) or 8 anchovy fillets in oil; one clove of garlic; a finely chopped mixture of: one spoonful of squeezed pickled capers and a handful of parsley; 5 spoonfuls of extra virgin olive oil (or a knob of butter)

Preparation: 10' - *Cooking time:* 15'

Sauté the garlic with the oil in a frying-pan, possibly made of earthenware, without allowing it to brown. Add the anchovy fillets and break them up on a low flame, stirring with a wooden spoon. Remove the garlic and add the chopped mixture, taste for salt and pepper, mix together well and take off the heat.

Excellent for stuffed eggs, for pasta* and for boiled beans* (add a little vinegar if they are black-eyed), it acquires flavour with the addition of a chilli pepper or a slice of onion.

Salsa verde

GREEN SAUCE

An abundant handful of parsley; one filleted anchovy (or a teaspoon of anchovy paste); one clove of garlic; one spoonful of well-drained pickled capers; 2 spoonfuls of pine-nuts (optional); the soft part of a bread roll soaked in two spoonfuls of red vinegar and squeezed; 6 spoonfuls of extra virgin olive oil; salt; pepper

Preparation: 30'

Chop the anchovy with the garlic, the capers, the parsley, the pine-nuts and the bread. Bind the sauce with the oil, stirring until it acquires a creamy consistency. Salt, lightly pepper and serve with boiled fish, boiled meat or calf's head, poached egg or boiled potatoes.

This extremely simple sauce also has numerous variations. There are those who advise mixing the parsley with other scented herbs (calamint, tarragon, rocket, basil...) or replacing the bread with a hard-boiled egg or a well-mashed boiled potato. And those, even, who add a few drops of meat concentrate or a spoonful of onion and the chopped yokes of a couple of hard-boiled eggs. For an ultra-fast variation, add to a cup of mayonnaise 3 spoonfuls of chopped parsley (or coriander, or tarragon).

Besciamella

BECHAMEL SAUCE

⚖️ 50 g of butter; 50 g of flour; half a litre of cold milk; half a teaspoon of salt; a pinch of pepper (optional); a pinch of nutmeg (optional)

⚖️ *Preparation: 5' - Cooking time: 20'*

⚖️ Melt the butter over a moderate heat in a thick-bottomed casserole dish without allowing it to brown. Add the sifted flour all at once and stir vigorously without allowing it to darken. Add the milk and stir again, taking care that lumps do not form (in which case you will need to pass the mixture though a sieve). When the sauce is smooth and creamy add the salt and pepper and, if desired, the nutmeg.

Maionese
MAYONNAISE

🌀 3 eggs at room temperature; 6 dl of extra virgin olive oil; half a lemon (or 6 spoonfuls of white wine vinegar); half a teaspoon of salt

🌀 *Preparation:* 20'

🌀 Break the eggs, carefully removing the white and the seed if it's there. Salt and for a few minutes mix slowly, always in the same direction. Continuing to mix in a harmonious and uniform way, pour in the oil a little at a time, making sure you allow it to be completely absorbed by the egg before pouring in any more. Before the mayonnaise gets too dense, dilute it with a few drops of lemon or vinegar. Taste for salt and lemon and serve. If you want to keep it for a longer timer, at the end add 3-4 spoonfuls of boiling water.

Sugo di carne
MEAT SAUCE

🌀 300 g of choice lean veal, in slices; 400 g of ripe tomatoes, cut into pieces, without skins or pips; a finely chopped mixture of: one onion, one carrot, one stick of celery; 6 spoonfuls of extra virgin olive oil; salt; pepper

🌀 *Preparation:* 20' - *Cooking time:* 1 h and 20'

🌀 In a pot, possibly made of earthenware, sauté the chopped mixture for about 15' on a low flame. Stir, making sure that the mixture does not burn. Add the meat and sauté it quickly; take off the heat, chop it up finely and put it back in the pot together with the tomatoes. Salt, pepper and simmer* for an hour with the lid on.

🌺 *Using the same method you can also prepare a tasty rabbit sauce.*

Sugo di salsiccia
SAUSAGEMEAT SAUCE

⌀ 300 g of fresh sausages, peeled and broken up; 400 g of ripe tomatoes cut into pieces, without skins or pips; half a red onion and a clove of garlic, chopped; 2 bayleaves (or a pinch of fennel seeds); half a glass of red wine; 4 spoonfuls of extra virgin olive oil; salt; pepper

⌀ *Preparation: 20' - Cooking time: 40'*

⌀ Sauté the garlic and onion in the oil, add the bayleaves and sausages and stir well. Bathe in the wine and add the tomatoes. Salt, pepper and cook for about 30'.

Salsa di pomodoro
TOMATO SAUCE

⌀ One kg of ripe tomatoes (*costoluti fiorentini* are ideal) cut into pieces, without skins or pips; one onion, one carrot and one stick of celery cut into thin slices; a few basil leaves; a bunch of chopped parsley; 6 spoonfuls of extra virgin olive oil, besides that needed for conserving; salt; pepper

⌀ *Preparation: 45' - Cooking time: 1 h*

⌀ Put the vegetables into a saucepan, salt and cook for about 40', gradually turning up the heat and pouring off the water of the tomatoes. Season with the oil, the salt and the pepper and put back on the heat for about 20'. Cool down and pass through a mouli. Pour the sauce into jars with an air-tight seal, together with a few basil leaves and cover with a dash of oil. Store in a cool, dark place.

Sugo scappato

RICH TOMATO SAUCE

ℰ⊙ 500 g of ripe tomatoes cut into pieces, without skins or pips; a finely chopped mixture of: one large onion, 2 carrots, 2 sticks of celery, a bunch of parsley; a bunch of basil leaves; half a glass of red wine; 4 spoonfuls of extra virgin olive oil; salt; pepper

ℰ⊙ *Preparation:* 30' - *Cooking time:* 45'

ℰ⊙ Soften the chopped vegetables in the oil and bathe in the wine. Add the tomato and basil, salt, pepper and simmer* for about 30'.

ℰ⊱ *The Italian name for this sauce, "sugo scappato" ("scappato" means "missing"), may derive from the absence of meat, being more of a "salsa" than a "sugo". For the same reason it is also called "sugo finto" (mock meat sauce). At the other extreme, there is a thick "sugo di festa" (party sauce), a very rich sauce containing minced meat, chicken breast, chicken livers and dried mushrooms soaked in warm water, to be added when the vegetables begin to change colour, that is before adding the wine and tomatoes.*

9

FESTIVE FOODS

Long biscuits and ring-shaped biscuits, women,
if you want them, ours are the finest
[…] do not wait for others to give them to you
just play the game and spend good money.

(Lorenzo the Magnificent,
Canti carnascialeschi, 15th C)

Traditional sweets are associated with festive occasions and each festivity has its own. Convents and monasteries were also specialized, not only in liqueurs, but also in sweets and preserves. Medieval sweets, made with honey, almonds, spices and cane sugar, were called *morselletti, bericuocoli, cialdoni* and *pinocchiati*, and were often served at the start of the banquet.
At Carnival time simple cakes were made, like *berlingozzo, stiacciata* or *cenci fritti*, though fair-grounds also sold *brigidini, roventini* and *mangia e bèi* filled with liqueur or syrup. Between Carnival time and Easter *quaresimali* were eaten and on Holy Thursday *pandiramerino*, decorated with cross-shaped cuts, were blessed. For St Joseph's Day there were *sommommoli* and *frittelle*, for the grape-harvest *schiacciata con l'uva*, in winter *pattona* and *castagnaccio*. Except for *zuccotto*, citrus-fruit tarts and trifles with liqueur or ice-cream, Florentine desserts are served with sweet sparkling white wines; dry pastries, *frittelle, cenci* and *schiacciata* are also eaten with balanced, light, sweet white wines like Moscadello, medium-bodied sweet reds like Aleatico and Morellino and, above all, Vinsanto.

Bomboloni
DOUGHNUTS

⚚ 200 g of flour; 30 g of melted butter;
15 g of brewer's yeast dissolved in half a glass of
warm water; 150 g of sugar; the grated peel of
half a lemon (untreated); a pinch of salt;
plenty of frying oil

⚚ *Preparation:* 45' and 3 h for leaving the
mixture - *Cooking time:* 30'

⚚ Heap the flour with a well in the middle
and mix in the sugar, salt, lemon peel, butter
and yeast. Vigorously work the mixture with
your hands to form a smooth, elastic ball, which
you should leave for 2 hours in a warm place,
covered with a flour-dusted cloth. Then roll
it out flat, 1 cm thick, and cut it with a glass
to make many discs (being careful to use up all
the scraps), which should be left to rise for
another hour between two floured cloths.
Fry them one by one in the hot oil, in which they
should float so as not to absorb too much of it.
Dry them thoroughly on kitchen paper and roll
them in sugar.

🐌 *As a disc or a ring, either plain or jam-filled,
cream-filled or chocolate-filled, doughnuts were once
made with flour, eggs and boiled potatoes. Krapfen,
more refined in taste though even heavier, are made
instead with eggs and milk.*

Cantucci
ALMOND BISCUITS

For about 40 biscuits: 500 g of '00' flour; 400 g of sugar; 250 g of sweet almonds, unpeeled and lightly toasted in the oven; 3 whole eggs and 2 yokes; one beaten egg; 50 g of melted butter; half a sachet of baking powder; a pinch of salt

Preparation: 30' and 1 h for leaving the mixture - *Cooking time:* 35'

Heap the flour with a well in the middle and add the eggs blended with the sugar, the baking powder, the butter and the salt. Work together quickly, add the almonds and mix again, in the end moulding long flattened strips, about two fingers wide and 1 cm thick. Lay them out, well apart, in a baking-pan lined with oven-proof paper and leave to rest for about an hour; then brush with the beaten egg and put them in a moderate oven for about 30'. Remove when hot and crunchy and cut into oblique slices 1 cm thick, which you can put back in the oven again for a light toasting. After cooling, they should be stored in an air-tight container.

Variations involve the flavour one may wish to confer to these delicious hard biscuits: half a small glass of Vinsanto, a teaspoon of grated orange peel, vanilla flavouring and saffron to colour.

Castagnaccio

CHESTNUT CAKE

🌰 300 g of chestnut flour; 50 g of sultanas soaked in warm water and dried; 50 g of pine-nuts; one spoonful of sugar; a handful of rosemary leaves; a glass and a half of cold water; 6 spoonfuls of extra virgin olive oil; a pinch of salt

🌰 *Preparation:* 10' in addition to the time for soaking the sultanas - *Cooking time:* 30'

🌰 Put the flour, sugar, salt and 2 spoonfuls of oil into a bowl. Pour in the water a little at a time, stirring well to obtain a fairly runny mixture with no lumps. Add half the sultanas and pine-nuts, mix, leave for 30' and pour into an oil-greased baking pan with a diameter of 26 cm, or into a typical rectangular baking-pan that gives the mixture a thickness of about 1 cm. Sprinkle with the remaining sultanas, pine-nuts and rosemary, pour on 2 spoonfuls of oil and cook in a hot oven for 30'. The cake is ready when the surface is brown, crispy and cracked.

🍂 *Castagnaccio has a very ancient history, and may originally have come from Lucca. In Casentino it is called "baldino", in some areas of the Florentine territory "ghirighio", in others "migliaccio". There are those who consider the thicker version (three fingers thick) more traditional, those who add walnuts and flavour it with grated orange peel, and those who omit the rosemary or even, when the flour is particularly good, the sugar.*
Pattona* is made with chestnut flour cooked for 10', without ever stirring, in a litre of boiling water with 2 spoonfuls of sugar and a pinch of salt. It is served warm, cut into slices, with ricotta or fresh pecorino.

Cenci

SWEET "RAG" FRITTERS

  300 g of flour; 50 g of melted butter
(or 4 spoonfuls of extra virgin olive oil); 2 eggs;
2 spoonfuls of icing or castor sugar; one spoonful of Vinsanto; the grated peel of one lemon
(untreated); a pinch of salt; plenty of frying oil

  Preparation: 1 h and 15' in addition to the
time for leaving the mixture - *Cooking time:* 30'

  Heap the flour with a well in the middle
and pour in the sugar, the salt and a little grated
lemon peel. Fold in the softened butter, the eggs
and the Vinsanto and mix until obtaining a firm
ball which should be left for about 30' in a cool
dry place. Then roll it out to about 2 mm thick,
and cut it, either with a knife
or a toothed pastry-cutter, into
lozenge shapes or strips. Fry
them in plenty of oil until
they become golden and
crispy, drain them and
dry them on kitchen paper
and serve them, hot or
cold, sprinkled with
icing sugar.

Frittelle di mele

APPLE FRITTERS

  300 g of rennet apples, peeled and cored,
cut into rounds 4 mm thick; a batter* of: 80 g
of flour, one spoonful of extra virgin olive oil,
one teaspoon of brewer's yeast dissolved in a
little warm water, a small glass of white wine
(or Vinsanto), a pinch of salt, 80 g of sugar,
one egg; plenty of frying oil

  Preparation: 20' in addition to the time
(1 h) for leaving the mixture - *Cooking time:* 30'

  While leaving the batter, which should be
fairly runny, prepare the apples (for a stronger
flavour, you can put them in an infusion with
more Vinsanto or in brandy). Dip them in the
batter, drain well and fry them in boiling oil.
Brown them on both sides, remove, let drip,
and dry on kitchen paper. Eat hot with a
sprinkling of sugar.

Frittelle di riso

RICE FRITTERS

ᐱᕋ 100 g of rice; half a litre of milk; 2 glasses of water; one egg; 2 yokes; a small knob of butter; 50 g of sultanas soaked in warm water and dried; half a glass of alkermes (or rum, or Vinsanto); one sachet of baking powder; 2 spoonfuls of '00' flour; the grated peel of half a lemon (untreated); a sprinkling of castor sugar; a pinch of salt; plenty of frying oil

ᐱᕋ *Preparation:* 20' in addition to the time needed to soak the sultanas and cool the rice - *Cooking time:* 40'

ᐱᕋ Cook the rice in the milk (diluting with water if it gets too dry) with the salt, butter, sugar and lemon peel. When the liquid has been completely absorbed, remove from the heat and leave to cool. In the meantime whip the whites to a froth. Add the yokes, the baking powder mixed with the flour, the liqueur and the sultanas to the rice; blend together well and finally add the frothed whites, folding in delicately. Fry by putting spoonfuls of the mixture into the boiling oil. Colour on all sides, remove, let drip and dry on kitchen paper. The fritters should be eaten hot and sprinkled with sugar.

ᐱᕋ *These are the classic "frittelle di San Giuseppe", which can also be prepared without the sultanas or the liqueur. Tradition has it that the rice should be cooked the evening before so that the following morning it crumbles easily. Using the same method you can also make fritters with semolino, flavouring them with orange peel as a pleasant alternative.*

Pandiramerino

ROSEMARY BUNS

300 g of white flour;
15 g of brewer's yeast
dissolved in a little warm
water; 20 g of sugar;
100 g of raisins; a handful
of rosemary leaves; 4 spoonfuls of extra virgin olive oil;
one beaten egg; a pinch of salt

Preparation: 30' in addition to the time for
allowing the mixture to rise - *Cooking time:* 30'

Heap the flour with a well in the middle
and pour in the yeast and the sugar. Mix until
forming a firm ball, which should be left to rise
in a dry place for about an hour until it doubles
in size. Add the raisins, the oil, the rosemary, the
salt, and knead them in.
Then divide the dough into rolls, which should
be left to rise for another 30' on a floured oven-
tray. Cut a cross into the upper part of each roll,
brush with the beaten egg (or a little oil) and
cook in a hot oven.

*A sweet-bread of extremely humble origin (typical
of Holy Thursday, when it was taken to be blessed).
Traditionally it was a large bread "enriched" only with
rosemary sautéed in a little oil, without sugar, without
egg, and only rarely with raisins.*

Quaresimali

LENTEN BISCUITS

100 g of flour; 100 g of sugar; 25 g of cocoa
powder; 25 g of hazelnuts ground in the mixer;
a pinch of vanilla; a pinch of ground cinnamon;
2 egg whites whipped into a froth; the grated
peel of half an orange (untreated); half a
teaspoon of baking powder; a small piece
of butter for greasing the tray

Preparation: 20' in addition to the time for
leaving the mixture - *Cooking time:* 10'

Mix all the ingredients together with the
whipped egg-whites, folding them in delicately.
Insert the mixture into a pastry-tube, a little at
a time, and squeeze out and draw well-spaced
letters on a lightly buttered oven plate. Leave
for one hour and cook in a low oven.

Schiacciata alla fiorentina

FLORENTINE FLAT CAKE

300 g of flour; 100 g of sugar; 100 g of lard; 20 g of brewer's yeast dissolved in a little warm water; one egg; 2 egg yokes; the grated peel of a small (untreated) orange; one sachet of vanilla; a pinch of salt; 50 g of icing sugar

Preparation: 30' and 3 h for the rising - *Cooking time:* 30'

Heap the flour with a well in the middle and add the yeast, working well until obtaining a fairly consistent mixture that should be left to rise, covered by a cloth, for one hour in a dry place. When it has swollen to twice its size work again (kneading well so as to incorporate air into the mixture), mixing in all the other ingredients except for the icing sugar. Lay the mixture in a greased rectangular oven-dish (it should be 2 cm thick) and leave it to rise for another two hours covered with a cloth. Cook in a hot oven. Leave to cool and sprinkle with icing sugar.

A Carnival sweet with an ancient tradition, also called "stiacciata unta" because of the lard (and, at one time, the pork scraps) which gives it a highly particular taste and consistency.

Schiacciata con l'uva
FLORENTINE FLAT CAKE WITH GRAPES

🌰 800 g of Canaiolo grapes, washed and dried; 300 g of flour; 20 g of brewer's yeast dissolved in a little warm water; 150 g of sugar; 2 spoonfuls of extra virgin olive oil; a pinch of salt

🌰 *Preparation: 20' and 1 h for the rising - Cooking time: 30'*

🌰 In a terrine mix the flour, the yeast, the oil, ⅓ of the sugar and the salt. Mix well and leave to rise for an hour in an open warm oven. Lay half the dough in an oiled rectangular oven-dish, cover with ⅔ of the grapes, half of the remaining sugar and a spoonful of oil. Cover with the rest of the dough, pressing well at the edges so that it sticks, cover with the rest of the grapes, the sugar and the oil and cook in a hot oven. The sweetbread is ready when the surface is golden.

🐦 *If you want it more fragrant, you can add a pinch of rosemary leaves or aniseed to the grapes on the top, or "inebriate it" with a generous dash of red wine before putting it in the oven.*

Zuccotto

ZUCCOTTO

🍥 For the sponge mixture: 100 g of flour; 100 g of sugar; 3 eggs; a grated lemon peel; a pinch of salt.
For the filling: 250 g of whipping cream; 250 g of sieved ricotta; 100 g of flaked dark chocolate; 50 g of candied fruit; 50 g of icing sugar; one spoonful of cocoa powder; 2 small glasses of brandy; one small glass of sweet liqueur

🍥 *Preparation:* 1 h and 30' in addition to the 5 h for cooling the mixture - *Cooking time:* 30'

🍥 Whip the eggs with the sugar for 15' until a soft, puffy cream is formed. Add the flour, the lemon peel and the salt. Mix well, pour into a greased and floured oven-dish and cook in a hot oven. While you are cooling the sponge-cake (to prevent it crumbling when being cut), whip the cream with the icing sugar, add the ricotta and divide the mixture into two unequal parts. Mix the candied fruit and the chocolate with the larger part, and the powdered cocoa with the smaller part, and cool in the refrigerator. Remove the crust and outer edges of the sponge-cake, cut it horizontally and make rectangular slices of sponge that will go to line the special cap-shaped mould (the *zuccotto*) and cover the filling. Brush the lining with liqueur, fill with one layer of cocoa cream and one layer of white cream, close by pressing well with more sponge-cake soaked in liqueur and put in the fridge.

🍮 *Although there are those who prefer a filling made with cream only, the ricotta confers a particular creaminess. Another variation involves replacing cocoa on its own with a syrup made of butter, cocoa and sugar heated for 5' in very little water.*

SIMPLE, BUT NOT EASY

Basic recipes

❦ Asparagus

Scrape the stalks of the asparagus, wash them, tie them together and cut the bottoms flat. Put them to boil, standing upright in a high, narrow saucepan with enough salt water to cover the white parts. Cook with a lid on for 15' if they are large ones, a little more if they are the wild variety. Remove from the heat, drain them, untie them, remove the white parts and dress them as desired.

❦ Batter

This is made in various ways, according to taste, to the type of ingredients to be fried, and to the lightness one desires.

For the fastest, to be used immediately:

150 g of white flour; a small cup of water; half a glass of lager (or half a sachet of pizza yeast); a pinch of salt. Dilute the flour in the water, beating with a whisk to prevent lumps from forming. Salt, add the beer, and possibly more water, until a liquidy, homogeneous mixture forms. For the most refined: beat 2 eggs with salt; add 150 g of flour and leave for about 30' before using.

For the most choreographic: use well-whipped egg-white only, which forms a kind of "cobweb" when fried.

≈ Beans

To make them with the skin tender but not over-soft, one must faithfully follow the tradition:

Dried beans (fagioli secchi)

Soak 400 g of beans overnight in cold water. Drain them and put them in an earthenware pot or a double-bottomed stainless steel saucepan with a clove of garlic, 3-4 sage leaves, 2 spoonfuls of olive oil, salt, a pinch of black peppercorns. Cover with 2 litres of water and simmer*, stirring occasionally, for at least 2 hours, adding salt when the cooking is done.

Fresh beans (fagioli freschi)

Shell 1 kg of beans and put them in a saucepan with 2 cloves of garlic, 3-4 sage leaves, 2 spoon-fuls of olive oil and one small tomato. Cover with plenty of cold water, add salt and put on the heat. As soon as it boils, lower the flame and simmer with the lid on for about 45'.

Flask-cooked beans (fagioli al fiasco)

400 g of dried beans (preferably *toscanelli*, but necessarily small so that they can be extracted after cooking) soaked overnight, 2 cloves of unpeeled garlic, 3-4 sage leaves, 5 spoonfuls of olive oil, salt, a pinch of black peppercorns. Put all the ingredients into a wine flask without the straw covering, fill it with warm water up to where the neck begins and seal it well with a flax tow. Then lay it in a nest of ashes and embers in front of a lit fire, though not so close that it breaks, making sure that the heat remains constant and turning it often for an even cooking; or, more simply, simmer it for a long time, wrapped up in a cloth, in a saucepan full of water. Adjust the salt and serve the beans seasoned with a sprinkling of freshly-ground pepper and a dash of olive oil. Try the tasty addition of finely sliced fresh spring onions.

≈ Boiled meat

See Broth.

≈ Broth

To make a good broth put the meat into cold water and simmer*; for good boiled meat immerse in boiling water. The meat should be of various types (lean meat, chicken breast, beef-steak cut-offs, ribs, loin, shoulder, rump, etc., half a tongue and a couple of bones): not less than one kg to be cooked for about 1 h and 30' in plenty of salt water together with a bunch of

aromatic herbs (parsley, celery, carrot, a piece of roasted onion; or also bayleaf, thyme, garlic, cloves) and two small tomatoes. Add half a chicken and continue cooking for another hour. Leave the meat in its broth for half an hour before serving (possibly with a piece of pig's trotter and/or head boiled separately; from their broth, filtered and cooled, a tasty jelly can be obtained) with pickles and green sauce, Tuscan mustard or oven-baked onions.

ᐓ Chickpeas
To make them with the skin tender but not over-soft, soak them for 24 hours in cold water with a spoonful of coarse salt; rinse under running water and simmer* for a couple of hours.

ᐓ Corn-meal
Simple spoonfuls of polenta accompanied by a good sauce of mixed meats, 'odori'*, dried mushrooms and tomatoes; or sausage with bayleaf and tomato, or pork ribs and mush-rooms. For the polenta, just sprinkle the corn meal into salted boiling water (2 litres per 500 g) and cook on a very low flame for 40', stirring fre-quently to prevent lumps from forming.

❧ Fricassee

A very delicate kind of stew (made with veal, but also with chicken, rabbit, lamb or mixed meats) sautéed in oil and butter and bathed in white wine. What characterizes the dish, however, and makes its preparation rather more demanding, is the sauce: 2 egg-yokes beaten together with the juice of half a lemon, mixed with the juices of the cooking after the pan has been taken off the heat so as to prevent the egg from setting.

❧ Fried cutlets

Take some good slices of sirloin weighing about 150 g each, beat them well to soften them and dip them into some beaten egg with a little salt. Then coat them in breadcrumbs, pressing to make them stick and shaking off any excess. Fry them in plenty of hot oil.

❧ Fritto

"Even a shoe is good if it's fried" goes an old Florentine saying, and the cuisine of the city confirms this with a sumptuous dish of peasant origin that includes: chicken, rabbit, brain, kidney, sweetbreads, lamb cutlets, courgettes and courgette flowers, sage, artichokes, mushrooms, aubergines, cauliflower and onions. Everything cut into pieces and dipped in a smooth batter (or dipped first in egg and then in flour or breadcrumbs) and, naturally, fried in very hot extra virgin olive oil to make it crispy.

❧ Misticanza

Simple, tasty salad made up of at least 4-5 types of wild greens and herbs (though the more the better), such as *terracrepolo, radicchio, salvastrella, lattughino* and aromatic *ruchetta*, dressed with extra virgin olive oil, salt and vinegar.

❧ Pasta

Tagliatelle, pappardelle, maccheroni, maltagliati and others are prepared by mixing: 400 g of flour;

2 spoonfuls of extra virgin olive oil; 2-3 eggs and a pinch of salt with enough cold water to obtain a smooth, elastic dough. Make a layer 1 mm thick and cut it into the chosen form.

ᴥ Pickles

With just a bit of knowhow, garlic, onions and shallots can be easily preserved.
The garlics, which should be large and fresh, must be peeled, put into an earthenware or dark glass jar so that the light does not change their colour, and covered with a good white wine vinegar. After a couple of days drain them, change the vinegar and add a pinch of salt, a pinch of black peppercorns and a few sage leaves. Leave for at least a month in a cool, dry place. The onions, instead, should be small. The best are Tuscan onions, whose form is slightly elongated. Peel them, put them in a glass jar, cover them with vinegar and red wine boiled together with salt, a pinch of black peppercorns, a few cloves, a piece of cinnamon, 2-3 bayleaves and a sprig of thyme. Cool, close the jar and leave for at least a month in a cool, dry place.

ᴥ Short pastry

Make a heap of 200 g of flour. In the middle put 100 g of butter in pieces, 100 g of sugar, 2 egg yokes, the grated peel of one lemon, a pinch of salt and mix rapidly with your fingertips.
You will obtain a smooth soft mixture which should be left for 30' in a cool place, wrapped in a cloth.

ᴥ Topini

This is the name, in Florence, given to potato gnocchi, which when homemade are nothing like the mass-produced ones that are bought in shops.
Boil 600 g of mealy potatoes with their skins (the cooking time depends on their size), peel them, mash them and leave them to cool. Then mix them with 200 g of flour, one egg and a pinch of salt until obtaining an even mixture. Make cylinders out of them 1 cm in diameter which you will then cut into pieces about 2 cm long. You can either use them like this or roll them on a grater, pressing slightly to produce the characteristic knurled finish. Cook in a large amount of salted boiling water, removing them with a skimmer as soon as they rise to the surface. Serve them with a tomato or meat sauce and a generous sprinkling of Parmigiano.

Useful things to know

Agresto (Sour grape juice)
The juice of grapes that have not fully ripened,
the bunches of small, hard, green, sour grapes
that are usually found on the highest tendrils.
Traditionally it was used instead of lemon and
vinegar to flavour boiled meats and sauces.

Arrosto morto
This is made by cooking meat in a pan, not on a
high flame, in olive oil and broth only. All the
other ingredients have been added over time.

Artichokes
Carciofi (from the Arabic *kharshuf*) became
established in Tuscany in the second half of the
15th century, especially the varieties known as
violetti and the large, tender *mamme*.
Carefully remove the hard outer leaves and the
fieno (hay) inside and immerse them in water
and lemon to prevent them from going black.

Ballotte (Boiled chestnuts)
Chestnuts cooked for at least an hour in lots
of water with bayleaf and wild fennel seed.
They are excellent with fresh ricotta and should
be eaten hot, freshly peeled and washed down
with a *vin novo* or Vinsanto.

Barding
An operation consisting of garnishing meat,
especially lean meat, with thin slices of bacon,
lard or ham to make it softer and tastier.

Battuto
This is the word for the *odori*, finely chopped
with a knife, a half-moon or a mixer, and used to
make the *soffritto* or to lard meat.

Bread
Whether the bread is dark due to the presence
of bran, or white, in Florence it is preferred with
a thick crust and rigorously *sciocco*, that is,
without any salt: perfect for tasty ham and salami,
it goes well with the intense flavour of crostini
paté and the aromatic herbs used in soups.

106

Broad beans

The Italian word *baccelli* means the fruits of legu-
minous plants (peas, beans, etc.), complete with
their pods and seeds. But in Tuscany this is the
word for broad beans: large and ripe those for
cooking, small and tender those for eating raw
with fresh salted pecorino cheese, known in fact
as *baccellone*.

Bruciate (Roast chestnuts)

"Slit" chestnuts (or *marroni*), that is, chestnuts
which have their skins cut, are roasted over a
fire, preferably a wood fire, in an iron pan with
holes in it, and are then wrapped in a woollen
cloth to keep them warm. If you want the
chestnuts *ubriache* (that is, inebriated), peel
them and soak them in *vin novo*, which is also
what they should be drunk with.

Cantucci (Hard almond biscuits)

Also called "Prato biscuits", after the town which
claims their recipe, invariably served at the end
of a meal with Vinsanto or Morellino dell'Elba.

Carabaccia

Onion soup thus called because the soup-bowl in
which it is served resembles the *karabos*, a Greek
shell-shaped boat. It is said that the famous *soupe
à l'oignon* derives from the Italian *carabazada* that
was introduced in France by Caterina de' Medici.

Cauliflower

To attenuate the bad smell it produces when
being cooked, I advise boiling it in water and
vinegar, and adding to it a piece of stale bread.

Cenci (Sweet fritters)

These strips of flour mixed with egg, fried and
coated in icing sugar, are found, with different
names, in many regions of Italy. In Florence
of old they were known as *guanti* or *crespelli*,
depending on the shape they were cut into.
Typical of Carnival, they are served with Vinsanto.

Chard

So that they retain all their flavour and goodness,
wash them and boil them without draining them
in a covered saucepan for about 10' without
adding water. The same goes for spinach.

Cibrèo

Delicate fricassee of chicken giblets, anciently served as an opening dish, today it is prepared rarely due to the difficulty of obtaining the ingredients for it: chicken livers, testicles, unlaid eggs, crests and wattles, sautéed in butter, sage and onion, bathed in white wine and sprinkled with chilli pepper. The name may derive from the Arabic *zingiber,* chilli, and *regius,* royal.

Crostini

Slices of stale bread 6-7 mm thick, toasted, moistened with broth and topped with sauces and pastes of various kind, and garnished with mushrooms, tomato, herbs, black olives, sausage and stracchino cheese. The bread (preferably household, though *fruste* cut diagonally can also be used) may be just stale, but also toasted or fried in olive oil or in butter, or even bathed in broth or Vinsanto; some may even prefer fried polenta as an alternative. Crostini of woodcock now belong to the realm of legend, though even spleen crostini are now becoming rare.

Cutlet

The name used in Tuscany is *braciola,* replacing the older *carbonata,* and is used to indicate meat on the bone cooked over charcoal. Today the word is used for a pork cutlet or a slice of veal without the bone, while *braciolina* is a thin cutlet and *bracioletta* a lamb chop.

Cuttlefish

To clean them you must remove not only the intestines and skin, but also the eyes, the beak, the bone and the little ink sac which must also be removed from squid.

Eel

To skin an eel, make a circular incision under the head. Then, holding the fish firmly by the head, tightly grip the piece of incised skin and pull it back over the whole body. Gut the eel by means of a long incision made along the underside and cut it into drum-shaped sections. If instead of a large eel you have smaller ones, cook them together with their skins.

Florentine cuts of beef

1 Giogo
2 Matamà
3 Collo
4 Sfaldatura del collo
5 Est. cotennotto
6 Soppelo
7 Cimalino di spalla
8 Bracciatello
9 Muscolo ant.
10 Sorra
11 Sodo di spalla
12 Int. mandorla del polso
13 Est. scoperchiatura
14 Costoline
15 Petto
16 Tasca

17 Contra
18 Falda
19 Lombata nella costola
20 Lombata nel filetto c.o.
21 Controfiletto e filetto s.o.
22 Cimalino
23 Rosetta
24 Groppa
25 Lucertolo
26 Girello
27 Campanello
28 Muscolo post.
29 Coda

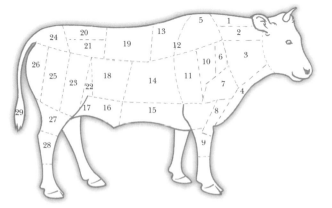

Gobbi (Cardoons)

The name given to sticks of cardoon due to their distinctive curvature (gobbo = curved, bent). After carefully removing the stalk, the upper part with leaves and the outer part with stringy threads, immerse them in water and lemon to prevent them from darkening. Then boil them with a little salt and a spoonful of flour so they retain their nice white colour.

Larding, piercing

A procedure consisting of making holes and incisions in lean meats in which to insert lard and aromatic herbs to flavour and soften them.

Maccheroni and pappardelle

Strips of homemade pasta (3 and 4-5 cm wide respectively) to serve with a rich game, duck or rabbit sauce.

Marinating

So that stews are more tender and tasty, lay the meat between two layers of aromatic herbs and chopped vegetables (carrots, celery, leeks or onions). Cover with white or red wine, adding vinegar for a more decisive taste or brandy, if you prefer it more mellow, and leave for 12-24 hours, turning every now and then. Drain the meat and sauté it, adding the liquid and the marinated vegetables during the cooking.

Meatloaf
To prevent it from breaking up during cooking, brush it with the white of an egg. To prevent it from crumbling when being cut, slice when cool.

Nepitella
In Florence this is the name for calamint.

Odori
The herbs and vegetables (carrots, onions and celery, but also garlic and parsley) used for the *soffritto* (the sauté).

Oil
A dash of Tuscan oil from the mill, strictly cold-pressed extra virgin oil, with a fine yellowish hue verging on green, with a full, intense flavour, pungent when *novo*, i.e. just produced, and indispensable for the perfection of every dish, sufficient on its own to embellish a fragrant slice of bread, a rustic soup and simple wild greens.

Oven
very hot:	200 °C
hot:	180 °C
medium:	170 °C
low:	160 °C

Panzanella (Bread salad)
One of the names for the old *pan molle* or *pan*

bagnato. Some say it comes from *zanella*, which described both the wayside verge on which countryfolk sat down to eat, as well as the basket in which women carried their food; others link it to *pantanella* (mud or slush), whose dampness and consistency it might resemble.

Pappardelle
See Maccheroni.

Pattona
In the past this mush of chestnut flour was used as an accompaniment for herrings and salt cod, scraps of pork meat and pork in general. A valid substitute for bread among mountain folk, during the last war it saved the Florentines from famine.

Pepolino
In Florence this is the name for thyme.

Pinzimonio
Raw vegetables that are dipped into an olive oil dressing.

Popone
In Tuscany this is the word for melon.

Ramerino
In Florence this is the word for rosemary.

Rosticciana
Pork ribs, cut into large pieces and roasted, preferably on charcoal, with salt and pepper.

Salt cod
In Florence prime quality salt cod can be found already desalted on Fridays. To consume it on another day, choose a good thick piece and keep it for at least 24 hours in a basin under trickling water.

Salumi
Strong-tasting without being piquant, Tuscan salumi are usually served with crostini as a star-ter, but can also be a savoury snack. **Prosciutto** is abundantly salty and peppery, and should be cut by hand into large thick slices. **Salame** is lean flesh with large rounds of fat, pepper, salt and the aroma of garlic; **finocchiona** or **sbriciolona** is coarsely-ground belly meat, with salt, pepper, garlic, spices and wild fennel seed; **carnesecca** is

the salted and peppered adipose tissue of the belly protected by hide, while **rigatino** comes from the more muscular part and gets its name from the layers of lean meat that stand out against the whiteness of the fat; **buristo** is pig's blood seasoned with spices, orange and lemon peel, fat and garlic, cooked in the pig's stomach, to be eaten fresh like **soprassata**, a mixture of head meat, tongue, fat and skin flavoured with garlic, lemon peel, salt, pepper, spices and parsley, boiled slowly, stuffed into a cylinder of raw cotton and tied carefully. Even **salsiccia**, made of well salted and peppered lean and fat chopped together, can be eaten raw on slices of dark bread; but try it also cooked for twenty minutes (after having been pierced with a fork) together with *fagioli all'uccelletto* or boiled turnip tops, chopped and sautéed in garlic and oil.

Scamerita
The part between the loin and the leg of the pig, veined with fat, which, when liquifying, makes the meat tender and tasty.

Sfumare
Bathe with wine and evaporate completely by cooking on a high flame.

Simmer
Cook very gently, so that the water, or the cooking juice just "trembles" at boiling point.

Singeing
This consists of passing over a flame farmyard chickens and rabbits and game to eliminate bothersome feathers and hairs.

Soffritto
The process of softening chopped *odori* in a little olive oil over a gentle flame.

Spinach
See Chard.

Squid
See Cuttlefish.

Tomatoes
Typical, and therefore recommended for almost
all recipes, are the *costoluti fiorentini*; but since
these are not always easy to find at the market,
they can be substituted with other tomatoes
suitable for sauces and even with tinned tomatoes.

Turnip leaves
Remove the hardest leaves, and strip the other
leaves of their central vein. To prevent them
from being bitter and indigestible, drain them
halfway through cooking and transfer them to
another saucepan of boiling water.

Tripe, rumen, reticulum, psalterium, abomasum
The various parts of the digestive apparatus of
ruminants are grouped under the generic term
"tripe". The abomasum, or *lampredotto*, looks like
a dark, curled ribbon; it is boiled and eaten hot
in a piece of bread, or used for soups and risotti,
or cooked with chard *in zimino*. The psalterium,
or *centopelli* or *foiòlo*, but also *libretto* or *millefoglie*
due to its numerous white folds, is used to
flavour soups. The smooth white *croce* is the
rumen, while the *cuffia*, with its characteristic
spongey appearance, is the reticulum. In
Tuscany only the rumen and the reticulum are
called tripe, whereas the other parts go by their
own name.

Zampa
Also called *zampetto* or *piedino di vitello* and, like
tripe, udder and head, it can be found already
boiled, with a great saving of time and effort. It
can either be stewed, or prepared plain with
butter, parsley, white wine and Parmigiano or
even just with butter, pepper and Parmigiano.

Zenzero
In Florence this is the word for chilli pepper.

Zimino
The name of a vegetable sauce. It is thought that
the word derives from the Arabic *semin,* made
with butter, or from *cimino* or cumin: rather
strange, considering these ingredients are not
even used.

INDEX

116

117

The main illustrations in this book:
On the cover: Anonymous 19th-century artist, *View from the Ponte Vecchio*, New York, Grassi Collection; p. 6: Miniature from *Specchio Umano* by Domenico Lenzi (14th century), Florence, Biblioteca Mediceo-Laurenziana; p. 8: Domenico Ghirlandaio, detail of the frescoes of the Cappella Tornabuoni, Florence, Santa Maria Novella; p. 13: Giuseppe Zocchi, *Night*, Florence, Prints and Drawings Room of the Uffizi; pp. 14-15: Telemaco Signorini, *The Old Market in Florence*, Montecatini Terme, Private collection; pp. 62-63: Giuseppe Zocchi, *View of the Arno from the Vaga Loggia*, Private collection; p. 101: Remigio Cantagallina, *View of Florence from Bellosguardo*, Florence, Prints and Drawings Room of the Uffizi.

THIS VOLUME WAS PRINTED
FOR NARDINI EDITORE
BY ALSABA GRAFICHE, SIENA 2009